THE TIMES

Changing your Career

Second Edition

practical advice to help you **MOVE ON**

sally longson

KOGAN
PAGE

First published in 2001
Second edition 2003

Kogan Page Limited
120 Pentonville Road
London N1 9JN

www.kogan-page.co.uk

British Library Cataloguing in Publication Data

A CIP record for this book is available from the British Library.

ISBN 0 7494 4104 6

Copy-edited, designed and typeset by D & N Publishing, Hungerford, Berkshire
Printed and bound in Great Britain by Clays Ltd, St Ives plc

Contents

Acknowledgements

My personal thanks to my publisher, Philip Mudd at Kogan Page, for entrusting me with this book, and my husband, Paul, and my family. Their wonderful support and interest has never waned.

Preface

Has your job become utterly soulless and devoid of meaning and satisfaction? Do you dream of escaping it and doing something more satisfying, exciting and rewarding? If this sounds familiar, then this book is for you. Whether you're simply playing with the idea of changing your career, or you're 100 per cent certain of what you want to do next and just need to get on with doing it, don't let any more time in your life go to waste thinking about it. Do something about it. This book will show you how, and will also explain why there's never been a better time to change career.

The fact that you're considering a career change provides you with an excellent opportunity to stop, think, take stock, and reflect on your needs and values both in and outside your working life. As you read through *Changing Your Career*, I urge you to throw your life up in the air and dare to live differently, as careers and lifestyles wave an ever-closer web and impact more on each other than ever before. Such a process will send you on a brainstorming blaze of self-discovery to work out where your niche lies in an increasingly complex and rapidly moving workplace. It may simply mean listening to your gut instinct, which is telling you to 'Stop! Get out of this job! Do something else!' as opposed to people you know saying, 'Oh, every job has patches like this. It will get better, honestly,' when in your heart you know that it won't. This book will help you build up a detailed picture of yourself so that you can pinpoint your new role in The Workplace.

The Workplace consists of a number of sectors which are all intrinsically linked, a bit like a huge jigsaw. It seems to grow ever more complex, with increasing numbers of pieces (opportunities), and so it seems to get harder to find the right spot to land on and work in. To help you find it, this book will help you build up a detailed picture of yourself. It will encourage you to think back to your past experience of life and put your memory to work, to recall things you felt strongly about or held a passion for, before others firmly suggested something more respectable, or safe, or acceptable to them.

Throughout this book, you'll come across boxes entitled 'Ask yourself'. They will help you identify what you want out of your new career, and consequently they appear in greater frequency in the first half of the book. Information is only power if you use it, so the 'Next Step' boxes will help you to use the self-knowledge you have acquired to move your thinking on, and to get to where you want to be. They are more numerous in the second half of the book. Summary tasks at the end of each chapter will help you move on to the next stage. Collectively, this information will help you decide what the next chapter of your working life holds.

Get yourself a notebook and jot notes down as you work your way through the various questions and tasks this book poses, so that you can build a fully comprehensive picture of yourself and move to a new career that's right for you. Your notes will help you boost your faith in yourself that you're doing the right thing, and create a strong sense of self-worth when you come to sell yourself to prospective employers.

One of the great things about changing career is that it's like going on a great adventure. I promise you that the opportunity to decide on and work for a new career will give you a tremendous feeling of enrichment and satisfaction, excitement and challenge. It will empower you more than you could ever imagine. It will also probably frustrate and worry you at times. This book will help you work through any 'Should I, shouldn't I?' and 'Am I mad?' moments you may have. It has, I hope, a very human touch.

Before we kick off, here are some ground rules to work from:

- Accept the past for what it was, dig information out of it, and move on. You can't change the past, but you can use it to impact on your future.
- When you're digging for information about yourself, go right back to your childhood. Conditioning as a child that we should meet the expectations of others – parents, the school, our friends – often prevents us from doing what we want.
- Be honest with yourself. Listen to your gut instinct.
- Give yourself time to work the whole thing out, but limit it, or you'll still be working it out when you draw your last breath.

- Don't be afraid to look for work that will be fun.
- Challenge yourself to be broad-minded and inquisitive.
- A new career could mean a new job, being employed by someone else. However, it could also mean that you start your own business. Look for opportunities, not just jobs.
- Expect to do some training and to learn a lot.
- Don't waste energy complaining about your current job. Put energy into doing something about it.
- If you decide to go with a career switch, promise yourself to see the change through. Remember, those who do make the switch often have just one regret, namely: 'Why didn't I do this years ago?' And lots of your friends, watching your progress from the sidelines, will probably wish they were on the same journey.

Ground rules over, let's get started...

1 *What is happening to you at work?*

I am always astonished at the number of people I've talked to – even casually, at the hairdresser, in the pub, on a train – who've switched career. Perhaps their first career wasn't what they were really looking for, or they chose to live a new lifestyle, which meant they had to change their job too. Others responded to a vocational calling which had become too powerful to ignore; or reacted to an event which forced them to sit down and really rethink their working lives. Many wanted to 'give something back' to society or mother earth by contributing to a cause they believed in while they considered they had the resources to do it: the energy, the contacts, the ability to learn and the conviction they were still marketable. Their stories are inspiring, because they had the 'get up and go' to make the change happen. Most did it by sheer graft and application. But they all found a way to switch from a working role that had become fairly meaningless to them to a career they valued and enjoyed. None of them had regretted their switch.

The joy of changing career is that the process is planned, driven and achieved by you for your own benefit. You own that process, and you set the pace (unless you want to prepare for some professional careers, when you are more likely to be at the mercy of professional bodies and academic institutions). If you succeed, you'll feel happier, more fulfilled, freer and stronger, because you've done it – you've made something happen for you. It will also make you more resilient in the workplace and increase your employability. It will broaden your skills base, extend your network of contacts and friends and boost your learning skills and ability to cope with change.

Of course, there are times when people have little choice but to re-evaluate their working lives and refocus. Press headlines remind us daily that economic, political and social trends impact hugely on the job market, alongside the current leaps effected in the technology and communications industries. For example, as financial institutions continue to merge, or take over other organizations, professionals will continue to find themselves employed one day, and without a job the next. To get work, those laid off will either need to be very mobile and to go to areas where such jobs continue to exist, or they will need to retrain to do something else. Other individuals change career as a result of personal circumstances or life events that have forced them to reconsider the way they work: perhaps a family illness, problems with childcare or the care of ageing parents. In the case of the agricultural sector, many farming families have turned to new ventures such as bed and breakfasts to keep the money coming in. A positive, open-minded, creative and 'can do' approach makes all the difference to those who have been forced to re-evaluate their working lives.

Now, you feel a need to rethink and refocus. But first, take time to consider whether this desire for change is about switching career – or whether there is something else in your life which you are not happy about and wish to change in some way.

ASK YOURSELF

What is happening in my life?
Is it just my career I want to change?

Before you plough into any decision to change your career, look at your life overall. Are there issues besides your career that you need to tackle? Pinpoint whether it really is your career that needs attention, or something else – a relationship, your image, the way you spend your free time, a desire to have more time with friends and family, the state of your finances or your level of fitness. If there are issues besides your career, they will contribute to the way you feel about yourself and your life.

Think, too, about what you want to achieve overall, and look at the 'Big Picture of Life'. Perhaps you're at a stage in your life when you're beginning to ask why you're here on earth and what the meaning of your life is, or maybe you're saying to yourself, 'Well, I've worked really hard since leaving university in my chosen profession. Now I want to relax and have more fun at work, and more time for other things.' So think:

- How has what you want and what is important to you changed in the last five years?
- How much of your day could you describe as doing things you really want to do?
- What goals or dreams do you have that you want to fulfil?
- If you were to be writing your autobiography at the end of your life, how would you want it to read? What would you want it to contain?
- How could you change your life for the better?

NEXT STEP

Tackle any issues you have in your life that are concerning you.

- Identify any areas in your life that you think require a new focus. Tackle them.
- Work out how you want to change them.
- Give yourself a timescale to work to.
- Be clear about how you'll achieve the change.
- Be specfic about the outcome you want as a result of tackling the issue.

If, at the end of the day, you have looked at the 'Big Picture of Life' and consider that it really is your career that needs an overhaul, there will be signs that you are right in looking for a change. You will find yourself saying things like:

- 'There must be a better way to earn a living than this.'
- 'My performance at work isn't what it should be.'
- 'Everything is such an effort.'
- 'I can't see any point in doing this any more.'
- 'I've done this for too long and once too often – it's time to move on.'

3

- 'Do I really want to still be doing this job next year?'
- 'I feel absolutely burnt out. I'd love to do something different.'

You may also find yourself turning to 'sickies' and self-awarded 'duvet days', late starts, lengthy lunches, the weekend and alcohol for comfort. You get angry with yourself because you are not doing anything about it and you get irritated, and snappy, and you are not sure why. Equally, you may wake up one morning and think, 'Well, I've had enough of this. It's been fun, but it's time to move on now. Time to do something different.'

If all this sounds familiar, start planning your exit before your performance and attitude really take a dive. Listen to what your gut instinct is telling you. Too many people don't listen to their hearts. We do so in many other areas of life – so why not at work? Frequently, it takes an incident at work – or even at home – to make people snap, and say, 'That's it. I can't stand this anymore. It's time to get out,' and to realize that's what their heart has been saying all along. So take control of your life, and start steering it in the direction

---

ASK YOURSELF

What is driving me to change my career?

---

you want. Find that missing element that puts meaning back into your working life, and which doesn't make you turn over when the alarm goes off, and think, 'Oh, no. Work. I wish it was Friday.'

'What's wrong with the job you've got, anyway?'

'Well, it's just not the same anymore. It lacks something…can't put my finger on it. Just doesn't mean anything to me anymore… it's not just the pressure of it all – it's something more than that. Something – well, deeper.'

Try to identify what is driving your desire to change career. Perhaps somewhere along the line, your current job lost a certain element that had made work meaningful, fun, and interesting. When you started, you may have considered your job to be a 'quality' one, worthwhile, enriching and satisfying. And then you started thinking, 'Well, I'll stick with it – it pays the bills, and I like my colleagues.' And now, you may have reached the point where you don't care about the bills and you can't stand your colleagues any longer. Look at your current job and ask yourself:

1. Why did I take this job, or choose this career? What appealed to me about it?
2. What difference do my efforts make to customers, clients or the organization? How does that difference matter to me?
3. How important do I consider the values and goals of my employing organization to be?
4. Why do I feel like a change now?
5. Do I have any idea about what I want to do next?

ASK YOURSELF

What sort of career change do I want?

In fact, you could change your career path – and lifestyle – by taking up any of the following options. Rank them in order of the strongest appeal for you at the moment:

- a new career – something totally and completely different _____
- to do a different job for the same company _____
- to take the skills I've developed to another sector _____
- to shift the emphasis of my current career _____
- to work for a charity which can benefit from my skills, at home or abroad _____
- to make major changes to my whole life _____
- to remain in the same line of work with a new employer _____
- to run my own business _____

- to buy a tried and tested business, like a franchise _____
- to do a mixture of things – like a portfolio worker _____
- to gain more responsibility at work _____
- to change culture and environment, but stick to what you know and enjoy _____
- to take a break, a rest – a sabbatical – to fulfil a personal goal _____

It is important to be sure that a career change is what you want, as opposed to a break, for example, because although the former can be achieved, it will take time, effort and determination.

'I really want to get out of my current career and switch to something totally different. But how difficult is it really going to be? What barriers and obstacles will I face?'

Changing career is not easy. Problems you may well encounter include:

- finding the time to do it;
- finding the energy to do it;
- financial commitments at home – house, children, mortgage, funding your lifestyle – wondering how you would cope on a reduced salary or level of income, if that's what your ideal career would involve;
- financial commitments at work – share options, pension plans, healthcare schemes;
- the crocodile boss, lurking in muddy waters to spy on your use of the company's phones, fax and e-mail systems, and whether you come into work later than usual looking as if you've just been to an interview;
- some careers – such as the armed forces – have an upper age limit;
- some sectors are considered to be chiefly a youth industry. The IT sector, for example, *appears* to outsiders to have a youth image, but in fact welcomes and needs people with experience from the workplace to add weight to their employee body.

Of course, you can create your own resistance to change by:

- Restricting your vision of the opportunities: 'There's nothing out there for me, that's the problem. I've looked in all the papers, nothing appeals.'
- Worrying what people will say not just when you bring the subject up, but afterwards: 'What if it all goes horribly wrong? My family think I'm mad, as it is, and I only said I was thinking about changing career.'
- Fearing the unknown: 'Oh well, it's much safer to stay where I am and work with what I know I can do. I'm sure things will get better. I couldn't cope with any more change.'
- Limiting the amount of training you are prepared to do: 'I want to be a vet. Is there a short course I could do? I've always looked after animals, so I've got lots of experience ...'
- Failing to focus proper attention to the process: 'Just one more glass of wine, and I'll make a start.'
- Refusing or feeling unable to adjust to a lower level of income – most of us could cut back on spending considerably if we had to: 'Cut back? Don't be silly. I overspend as it is now and you are suggesting a swap to a job with a lower income?'

ASK YOURSELF

Have any of the following seriously put me off changing career in the past:

	Yes/No
Fear of change	____
'I'm too old to change. Better to stick to what I know.'	____
Family criticism	____
Stepping into the unknown	____
Fear of doing the wrong thing	____
The thought that 'Maybe it's just me and things will get better.'	____
Letting people down, eg your parents	____

Thinking that you'd never cope financially _____
Fear of failure _____
Lack of confidence in your ability to do it _____
No qualifications or wrong range of qualifications
for the job you want _____
No clue of what to do next _____

NEXT STEP

Learn from the past. And then look forward.

Knowing why you may have put off changing your career
before will help you be alert to any possible obstacles you
might create in your journey to switch career.

You can overcome many of these points if you are determined and
focused enough, even if your career change means revamping your
life. Use your vision and imagination to help overcome them. Some
career changes take little time to achieve, others far more – that
depends on the sort of switch you want and what qualifications and
experience you have acquired to date. But just think, what would
your life be like if you had a job you loved doing for 48 weeks of the
year? Think creatively, but be realistic. Are you prepared to train for a
new career that might hold greater value and meaning for you, but
mean a reduced salary? Are you happy to take a long-term view of your
career change, using a couple of stepping stones, perhaps over several
years, to get to where you want to be?

It is possible to change – more so now than ever before

Chapter 3 delves in more detail into the circumstances that are
providing the opportunity for people to switch career but, in the
meantime, rest assured that:

- Career paths don't exist any more – you create your own.
- What is important is the way you prepare yourself for your new career and sell yourself when it comes to landing a job.
- There are more opportunities to train for a new career, and you don't even have to attend college.
- In many careers, 'Experience of Life' is deemed a 'Very Good Thing'.
- There's a wider range of careers and ways to work now than ever before.

Don't let yourself make excuses not to change career

The excuses for putting off a career change are endless, and some are particularly career-related. They may sound familiar.

'It's not a good time to do it.'

Don't let yourself fall victim to procrastination by saying, 'Oh well, I'll do it next year.' At that time, you'll decide it's too late to change career and you haven't really got time anyway because you're far too busy with the kids, your mother-in-law's health isn't too good, enjoying yourself, coping with a ridiculous work-load…There's no time like the present!

'I can't think of anything else to do, really.'

Many of us are so immersed in the working environment around us, it is really quite hard to think of the jobs and careers other people do. The pressure and pace that many of us face at work today makes it very difficult to visualize how the rest of the workforce goes about its business. So it is hardly surprising that when you make a half-hearted attempt to consider what else you might do in your working life, fleeting glances at the evening paper do not inspire you. Don't start off on your career change by looking down recruitment pages in the press. Start by building your knowledge of yourself. To make a wise career move, you need to know first what you want in a job. Identify what you want to apply on the job, in terms of the skills, knowledge and qualities you want to use, and the people you want to work with, and finding the right niche in the mass of careers and opportunities out there becomes much easier.

Consider, too, how often you reflect on all the opportunities available to you. When you walk down your high street, or through the shopping mall, for example, do you know how many of the stores in there are franchises? Become alert to the opportunities available along your main street, instead of walking past blindly. Talk to people about their jobs, and find out how they got into them. Build up one picture of yourself, and another of the workplace, and eventually a way to merge the two will come to you, and you will know what your new career is to be. You can in fact create your own working opportunity, which fits your interests and needs.

'I've only done this all my working life; it's all I know. I can't do anything else.'

Top Tip

'I can't do anything else'
You *can*.
You can learn to do something else.

Career change is all about learning and retraining for a new trade, a profession, a new craft, occupation, or role. Fortunately there are a multitude of ways to learn, from the traditional adult education evening classes, to distance-learning programmes, often online at a time which suits you... when the children are in bed, your partner is watching *Match of the Day*.

Top Tip

Recognize the need to train, learn and prepare for your new career, possibly in your spare time.
You can't move from one career to another without doing something.

Rest assured that:

- Governments recognize that people will need to change career as their own personal aspirations shift and the workplace continues to undergo a massive transformation. Together with education and training providers, successive governments have implemented a range of initiatives and programmes to respond to such changes, enhancing the opportunity to switch career.
- It is never too late to learn. Visit www.waytolearn.co.uk and be inspired by success stories from people who've done it!
- There are more ways 'in' to a profession or job now than ever before – you pave your own career path. You won't necessarily have to study on a full-time basis.
- Many skills, such as handling difficult people, transfer from one career to another.
- Learning as an adult is very different to studying as a child. However well or badly you did at school, you can wipe the slate clean and start again as an adult.

'I think I was a complete failure at school. How can I go back to education now?'

If you did badly at school, ask yourself why. Do any of these reasons figure among your failure to achieve, succeed and stand out from the crowd?

- lack of school expectation of the students;
- you lacked ambition or a clear career goal;
- you couldn't see how what you were learning would be any use at work, so didn't bother;
- poor teachers and facilities;
- lack of parental encouragement and support;
- basically, you were a typical teenage rebel and other things seemed a lot more fun and more important, like a good social life and not being the class 'swot'.

Going back to train and educate yourself as an adult is a completely different scenario. You're learning because you want to. You're learning for *you*.

Top Tip

If your brain feels rusty, reboot your brain power.
Get into the habit of learning again.
Choose a course which interests you – let your
heart choose your course.

'There's no advice out there! No one to help the adults... it's all geared to young people.'

Careers practitioners recognize that, in an ideal world, every person would have access to lifelong careers guidance. After all, many of us use financial advisers and life coaches to help us make the most of our money and time. Governments acknowledge that there is a need for lifelong access to careers guidance for everybody, but they are hung up in the debate as to how to provide and fund it. Don't wait for them to come up with an answer –they will still be debating when you totter into retirement.

But many people don't use careers advisers to switch career. They work through the process on their own with the help and support of friends and family. Where appropriate, they contact people who could help or advise them on specific issues, such as financial help for retraining, interview technique, or a general overview of the sector. There is a lot of help if you reach out for it, and there is plenty of information, which this book will guide you to.

Be ready to leave the past behind and to move on to your future

If you have been with one company for most of your working life, you may have developed an ingrained sense of belonging which makes it harder to move on and leave the past behind you. The relationship between employer and employee has changed beyond recognition. Neither can rely on each other for loyalty and lifelong commitment. Learn to let go of company loyalty, and to put yourself first.

> I changed career and I wished I had done it earlier. Don't waste your time, money and energy doing things you don't enjoy because of some misplaced loyalty.
>
> Lee

ASK YOURSELF

How far is my current job draining my resources?

In any given week, you have 168 hours of time and life to play with (seven days **x** 24 hours). Look at the way you spend your week. If most of us spend 40 hours a week at work ('And the rest!' you are probably shouting at me indignantly) for example, and extra time preparing for work, thinking about it and making the journey in, it's no wonder the quality of your job affects other areas of your life. Ask yourself how much of your time accounts for your current job. Don't forget to take into account that de-stressing time you need at the end of the day. Does your job leave you too exhausted to do anything, other than slump in front of the television, wondering whether you should apply for *Who wants to be a millionaire*?

Work costs us money, too. We pay tax, and national insurance. Most of us pay for our journey to work. We need money while we are there: leaving presents, birthday presents, lunch, dressing the part, attending social functions and belonging to the right organizations. Ask yourself how much your current job costs you every week. How much longer are you prepared to put your money, time and energy into doing something that you do not enjoy or find satisfying anymore?

13

NEXT STEP

There will always be a time to move on, so seize it:

1. Recognize *your* time to move on; and what's behind your motivation to change.
2. Do something about it.
3. As you contemplate your working life, consider the sort of lifestyle *you* want; the skills and abilities you want to use, and the kind of relationship you want with an employer.

Summary exercises

1. What excites you about the prospect of changing your career? What are you most looking forward to?
2. What benefits do you think you'd gain?
3. Rank your current job on an enjoyment scale of 1 to 10, 10 being the most enjoyable. If you could introduce anything to it to make it a 10, what would that something be?

If you want to change career, you can.
If you really want to change career, you will.

---

2 *People do change career – it can be done*

You only have to read the press and watch the news to see that there is no more job security, and that the only way to heaven on the career front is by striding purposefully through the jungle of change and creating your own path. Every day, the papers are full of stories of mergers, acquisitions, companies downsizing, restructuring and closing down. Equally, you will note there are plenty of stories about jobs being created, new businesses starting up and initiatives announced to help people retrain. Surrounded by such events, it is no surprise that more and more individuals are waking up to the fact that they do not have to wait for change to come to them. They are going after change themselves and not waiting for employers to shape the future for them.

These days, your life overall will have far better quality if you can create and plan your own journey through its maze of choice and opportunity, because you'll be making decisions based on what's important to you. To a considerable extent, you have already done that throughout life, by making choices such as:

- the subjects you chose to study at school or college;
- the university you went to;
- the summer jobs you have enjoyed;
- the career you chose to follow or the first full-time job you had;
- the hobbies and interests you have delved into;
- the employers you have chosen to work for;
- the areas you decided to settle in;
- the people you choose to spend your free time with;
- the way you spend your free time.

ASK YOURSELF

What can I learn from the decisions I've
made in the past about the values I hold?

---

1. What appealed to you about the choices you made?
2. Who and what influenced your choices? How much
   influence did your own thoughts and beliefs carry?
3. How important have career and lifestyle considerations
   been in the decisions you have made throughout your life?
4. What have you learnt about yourself from these choices?
5. What did you naturally veer towards?

What you valued and wanted most lay at the bottom of each
decision you made (unless it didn't matter that much at the time);
this is especially the case where your hobbies and interests, and the
way you spent your free time, were concerned. After all, you're the
person who really knows what makes you happy, and who wants to
be unhappy doing things they don't want to do in their spare time?

NEXT STEP

Identify the values that lay at the bottom of your decisions. Keep
them in your mind as you plot your new career.

Frequently, the career changes individuals make today are driven by
non-work influences as much as work ones. This chapter will show
you how people at different stages of their careers and lives came to
decide to switch career, and how these changes have impacted their
jobs and lifestyles.

'I started work, but the job wasn't really right. So I changed career.'

Childhood conditioning and expectations, drummed into us by parents and schools, often prevent us from doing what we really want. 'I went into it to please my parents' must be one of the most frequent phrases careers officers hear; and yet all parents claim to want is for their children to be happy. 'They've put so much into supporting me,' claims many an undergraduate, 'that I just can't let them down.' Fears that parents would sulk or suffer major disappointment if you fell out of the 'respectable' profession or job they were so pleased and proud you went into, can create tremendous personal resistance within you to making a change at all. The desire to meet the expectations of family and society at large can influence early career decisions, so that many of us end up doing what we feel we should do, rather than what we want to do. Too many people then stay in jobs they dislike because they fear stepping outside of society's expectations and making the break with what other people regard as 'normal'. But now there is no such thing as 'normal'.

Many people go into a job because it was the first thing they were offered, and at the time they just wanted a job, either to stop everyone asking them, 'So what are you going to do after university, then?', or to make the problem of deciding what to do actually go away altogether. Many graduates 'temp' for a while to repay loans and debts, and obtain experience about which to write on a CV. A year later, they are stunned and a bit embarrassed to realize they are no further forward in finding that right job or even thinking about it. Others go for a career or profession which has a clear training route, such as teaching or accountancy, that does not demand a lot of research to be able to say, 'Yes, that's right for me'. Then one day, they wake up to realize that, 'No, this really isn't right for me at all,' and think, 'But how am I going to admit that and get out of it now?'.

As a result, many people feel on a different wavelength to the job they are employed to do, because their job doesn't relate to what they deem to be important. At first, that does not necessarily matter, because perhaps they drifted into it on the 'something is better than nothing, and at least I'll get experience' basis, without relating their values and beliefs to the workplace. A classic example is the

17

university graduate who drifts into teaching for all the wrong reasons – it is a fairly secure job, it pays the bills, a postgraduate course takes only a year, you get plenty of holidays and time to think about what you really want. These values lie very far from the real motivations required to be an excellent teacher: to bring the best out of all the youngsters in your charge and help them realize their potential. It begins to meet solely the necessity to bring in a pay cheque at the end of the week and the human need for company. But as the invincibility of youth begins to fade, and you realize that life is really something very precious after all, feelings of frustration hit home and the idea of changing to work which is more meaningful or fun begins to make itself heard more frequently and increasingly loudly. Life becomes too short to waste time doing anything else.

It takes courage to admit that your role in the workplace isn't right any more, firstly to yourself and then to others, but you will probably feel a range of emotions once you have done so. A tremendous relief and a funny feeling of being lost, and 'Where do I go now?' are quite normal. Sit down and have a good, hard, *serious* think about what it is you really want to do. Don't expect to achieve this in a few days or weeks. Take time to reflect on your experiences at work – even those summer jobs you had as a teenager. Talk to friends and family friends about their jobs, and what their day *really* involves, and find out what it is like working in their sectors. If they are blissfully happy in their jobs, ask them how they came to find such a niche. Assess what is not right with your own current role, and you will be in a stronger position, firstly to understand why, and secondly to explain it to others, family, friends, and prospective employers.

If you have drifted into a role after graduation, and don't think it is right for you, don't lose faith in your prospects. All experience comes in useful at one time or another in life. Many employers – including large professional companies – recognize that young people and graduates do sometimes stray into jobs or companies that are not quite right for them, but who nevertheless pick up useful skills and experience, and not least an idea of how a business func-tions. In fact, some companies deliberately pick up graduates with a couple of years' work experience, as opposed to the graduate fresh out of university or college, so that they take on people who are no longer raw material, but who have acquired a good idea of what work is all about.

If you study the local paper and national press recruitment pages, you will see headlines such as, 'Frustrated in your present job?' from all sorts of different organizations, many of which want to recruit people with experience from another industry. These companies will want to see a track record of achievement in your life to date, but they understand that you want to '*call time*' on what you are doing at the moment. Know what you are looking for in a job and what you can contribute, and do your research to prove you're serious. You'll sell yourself far more effectively.

'How do I tell people – I mean, my family and friends?'

For many people, this will be a major worry. Be clear about what it is about the work that you are not enjoying, using specific examples to make your point. Show them how you have given yourself a chance to like the damn job. People who still say 'Oh, you just haven't given it a chance,' or 'I'm sure it is just a bad patch; everybody goes through them, you will see,' have got the subtlety of a steamroller. Perhaps they are not listening to you properly (you have to ask yourself if they ever really did), or they have little or no understanding of what it is like to be at work. To spend your working life doing a job you loathe, often under great pressure from the boss and customers, will guarantee you a miserable life, especially when you know you have the option to get out. For many of us, our family background, formal education and experience of work form a considerable influence on our career decision-making process. Maturity, together with a knowledge of what works for us and what doesn't, gives us the confidence to admit when things are not right, even when we know we will have to do some awkward explaining when we announce that to family, and to do something about it. Which individual in their own right mind *wants* to spend the next x number of years doing a job they dislike, just because somebody might disapprove?

'I wanted to move up the career ladder. I just wasn't reaching my full potential at work.'

I could tell I was reaching a plateau in my job. Everything was such an effort. I was fed up of it. I wanted to take off and travel for a few months and do something with more bite when I got back. I went off to Chile to travel for six months, came back, and successfully applied for a management training position with a retail chain. I've joined the Institute of Management and go to local events, and I'm studying for professional qualifications. I wanted to do more with my working life than just drift along. I wanted to start contributing to the direction of something. My travels overseas gave me the confidence I needed and the kick up the backside to do it. Other things in my life will have to go while I'm studying and working for the qualifications – but I know it will be worth it.

Antoinette

Some people coast along for years, biding time, collecting the monthly pay check or weekly wage packet. Then something happens which makes them realize they can either keep coasting, or shift up a gear into management, or move into a more specific area, perhaps specializing in something they find they're good at and enjoy, like information technology, training, human resource development or marketing. This in turn can lead to a new career at a different level – often with the same company.

It takes work to move up the corporate ladder, and you'll need to demonstrate:

- achievement and performance;
- experience;
- strong skills, not least emotional intelligence;
- knowledge of your sector and how it can be affected by external and internal factors;
- qualifications – as you aim higher, you may need professional qualifications such as an MBA or similar;
- ambition, drive and tremendous focus – a hunger to succeed.

You'll need to give your career a massive injection of time and loving care, and be very, very focused. People at the top are. They don't waste a minute. Be inspired by Sarah Brown's book, *Moving On Up* (see Further Reading), which tells the story of successful people in various sectors in the UK, who has inspired them along the way; and their advice for people starting out reach the top in their fields.

You can also take your skills and experience off to another sector where the culture is totally different:

I'd worked in management for a retail bank for 17 years, and it was becoming obvious that there weren't more senior positions I could go for without putting in the most obnoxious hours and being even more competitive. At 37, I'd better things to do and I felt my bank had already had a good share of my life, so I asked about early leavers schemes and took off. My colleagues were all hugely envious. I was intending to have six months off, to travel, but I saw the opportunity to work for a cancer charity, running a local unit. My father had died of cancer and I saw this role as an incredible way to give something back, without having to do any hands-on nursing. It has given me a chance to lead others, and to develop new skills in fund-raising, and my networking abilities have proved to be really useful. The money is far less than I was on, but that doesn't matter – the satisfaction I get from the work outweighs anything money could bring me.

Adrian

'Something happened in my life which made me think and make some changes.'

The desire to change career may come upon us very suddenly; we wake up and think, 'There's got to be more to work than this.' This happened to Sean: 'Something told me it was time to leave. It was really weird. I didn't even question what my heart was telling me. I just knew it was time to go, and do something different. I needed a new start.' Many people are spurred on by events which have a major impact on them – the death of a loved one, the break up of a relationship, an accident which leaves them feeling they were lucky to survive and they've been given another chance, almost a second life, if you want to call it that. Tragedy or shock often gives people the strength and the jolt they need to turn their lives around and sit down and work out what they really want from life and to develop the motivation to make it happen. This is particularly the case as we get older and see others retiring and dying, often having talked about the regrets they had about their lives, and saying, 'Don't make the same mistake I did. You *can* change, you know.'

My husband left me, and after that my world would have fallen apart anyway, so I decided to chuck everything in and go after something

21

I'd wanted for a long time: becoming a lawyer. I went to university as a mature student, did my Common Professional Examination for a year, trained, qualified and now I'm hoping to specialize in matrimonial law, so I'm studying a part-time postgraduate degree. I had to give my dream career a go because otherwise I'd be wondering for the rest of my life whether I'd have ever made it – and I couldn't live with that. At the time John left me, things couldn't have got worse than they were in my life – the only way was up. And I realized that only I could change my life – nobody else could do it for me. I found a determination and strength that I never knew I had. I've acquired a professional status, a new challenge, a totally different lifestyle and a feeling of worth. I suppose I've found a new *me*, really.

Meagan

People like Meagan find they need to acquire a sense of purpose in their lives. In part, people who want to change career are often seeking the answer to that enormous question, 'What am I doing here?' or want to recreate their lives with something they value. In Meagan's case, her self-esteem rocketed.

'One of my friends is turning what started out as an interest into her new career.'

Current or new interests can lead to a new career while you are still in your old job:

In my job as an insurance broker, I found myself increasingly bored with the paperwork and having to deal with frantic, worried people on the phone all day. I'd always loved working out, and had a natural interest in fitness, so when my local gym said they were running weekend courses for people who wanted to be fitness trainers, I applied. My life has changed dramatically. Instead of watching television or clubbing, I spend my evenings studying and teaching aerobics at a local club. I'm developing a network of customers, who attend my classes. Actually I think I want to get into health promotion, and I'm going to approach several local organizations to see if I can work for them. I've got to make sure I talk to the right people and get myself known – I'm just waiting for the right opportunity in health promotion to come my way. Then I'll give in my notice at the insurance company.

Rhona

Rhona is making her career goals happen because she is taking control of her own development and training; she is networking to promote her skills and get herself known so that when she is ready to start her own business, she has some support behind her. She is researching the needs for fitness trainers in her locality and is trying to find a niche in which she can become an expert, which will make her that little bit different to other fitness trainers. Finally, she is focusing on achieving her career goal and won't let anything get in its way.

> My friends have been really supportive, although I don't see so much of them at the moment. On my birthday, they all turned up unexpectedly in one of my classes and got everybody to join in a rousing chorus of 'Happy Birthday', once the class was over. You need positive people like that to help you through the career change process.

Peter also developed an interest into a career. He had taken photographs since he was at university. He often helped out at important family occasions – christenings, weddings, anniversary parties – and he had been developing his own business in this niche area while still teaching in secondary school. He developed a freelance business, where his maturity and ability to make people laugh and to relate to a wide range of people proved to be a tremendous asset. He attended a course in running his own business at his local college and spent weekends doing parties and events in the holidays to build up a name for himself while he still worked during the week. He found a niche in his area and set out to become an expert in it.

> My lifestyle has changed, because I work most weekends, now – it is when many weddings are. I tend not to go out on Friday and Saturday nights because I need to be fresh and alert the next day. If I'm hungover, it shows in my photographs and the way I handle people. The plus side is that I'm not restricted to going away in the school holidays anymore, as I was when I was teaching. It is very rewarding

work – I'm now finding I do a wedding for a couple and then they ask me back a year or so later to do the christening.

Peter

Others take on roles that strongly relate to their hobbies and interests, but demand a less 'hands-on' approach, as John did. An accountant for 30 years, John retired early when his firm downsized. Shortly after, his local golf club approached him. John had been an enthusiastic player for years and knew most members of the golf club quite well. The club wanted someone to handle the business side of the club – and they'd thought of John. 'The books, you know, no rocket science stuff,' they told him. 'A few mornings a week, a small salary. Would you be interested?' John accepted and enjoyed his new role. He used his brain, kept in touch with new legislation and played an increasingly important role in the business direction of the club. John's open-minded approach helped him find a job where he felt appreciated, and he also was able to fit a round of golf in far more regularly. His new role helped him cope with a major change in his life – retirement – and handle the stress of leaving a company he had worked for for over 30 years.

Going for a lifestyle move

My partner and I always wanted to live in the country and run our own business. When we saw the cattery advertised for sale, we went to have a look at it out of madness, really. The couple we bought the cattery from had run it in their fifties as a second career. We did a course in running your own business and cattery management. We've combined the cattery with a franchise pet food delivery service. Our main problem is getting away for a break – even a day. But the bit I enjoy is driving the business forward ourselves – I'm fairly creative and love thinking up new ideas to develop the business and make it more profitable. My partner is better at the administrative tasks. And we both love handling the cats and dealing with people. The level of responsibility surprised us both – you don't think there's much when you are working with animals, but pets are children to some people – their special prized jewels. So it's a good combination of skills and abilities – and it has given us a totally new lifestyle.

Peter

There are plenty of opportunities for people wanting to make a lifestyle move. Buying a franchise or an existing business can be a good way to go from being an employee to boss. The Web site www.daltons.co.uk can help you search out businesses such as pubs, inns, small guest-houses and post-offices (and check your local newsagent for the Daltons newspaper). If you prefer to buy into a larger, branded and supported business, such as McDonald's, then visit www.british-franchise.org.uk to find out more. If you choose a good franchise, then the risks are considered lower than setting up your own business.

Lifestyle moves need to be researched thoroughly, because it is easy to glamorize how the other half lives. Find out how life will differ by talking to the locals and spending time in the area you plan to live in doing your research. How would you cope with country living without the take away or delivery service, the second post and the ability to walk down to the local shop for the paper? And do not forget to consider living costs. Wages and salary levels differ throughout the UK. That said, staying where you are and becoming your own boss could change your entire lifestyle.

'I've just been made redundant. What next?'

'I think I'm going to be pushed, and I want to jump before they push me – I want to turn the whole thing on its head...'

My pharmaceutical company offered me redundancy from my position, or a job which didn't appeal at all. I took the package offered, which gave me the money I needed to retrain as an aromatherapist. It was a risk – I had no guarantee that I'd pass the course, or get a job at the end of it. But I did pass, and decided to set up my own business, working from home. I suppose the easiest thing would have been to take another job in human resources with another company; but I'd been doing safe stuff all my life and wanted a change – I could always go back to it if my new career didn't work out, although I didn't tell anybody that. Anyway, a career development loan helped me to finish the course. Having been in such a stressful environment myself, I really love helping other people cope with their stress levels and enabling them to relax. I feel much happier.

Sheelagh

Redundancy. Ouch. Even if you're expecting it, it comes as a shock. You may feel a number of things – hurt, resentful, lost, overjoyed. Try to handle situations in which you're pushed to go in a positive light – easy to say, I know – and regard them as an opportunity to change. Don't rush into anything. If you've been made redundant, you may be offered careers counselling as part of your package. Take it. Go determined to make the most of it, else you're wasting part of your package. It's yours to make use of. You may be able to use any pay-off to retrain for another career, to take time out to travel or do voluntary work.

Redundancy offers people the opportunity to reassess their life goals and career aspirations. Learn how to handle such a process, unbelievable and numbing as it is at the time. Develop emergency exits to handle such a situation should it occur – you'll find it far easier to cope if it happens again. And if you're watching jobs disappear all around you in your sector as it contracts, maintain a positive air, but start planning your next step. Re-evaluate your career to date and assess what you want to do next before you start looking for work. Time out can be more useful than you think, if you can organize your finances. If you owe money to banks or credit card companies, tell them what's happened to you if you have been made redundant, and look for ways to economize. Money has a habit of running out far more quickly than we think it will. We can all now expect periods of time in our lives when we're not working, and financial service providers are waking up to the fact and offering products to help people through times like these.

You may have been forced to relocate, thanks to your partner's job. Use your time to see what you can get out of it by rethinking your career – and even your life. If your partner has been asked to relocate, see if you can get his or her company to pay for you to retrain for another job, or see if it will pay for careers counselling for you to have a fresh start, as part of the relocation package.

Some people change to fit in with family circumstances or their own personal reasons, such as health

Many people adjust their working lives to fit in with changing circumstances at home, and indeed this is one of the major reasons women are setting up their own businesses. Fear of illness, or sickness within the family, can force people to revisit their career and plan for greater job security in the future, especially if they are the main breadwinner as Jenny was:

> I'd been a nurse for years, but that came to a halt when I injured my hip too much to do it anymore. I found my new career through good fortune and chance, really – I was in the right place at the right time. I'd always enjoyed making dresses. I'd made a dress for a friend who was going to a wedding, and she got lots of favourable comments on it and people started ringing me to see if I could do the same for them. I set up my own business from home and now concentrate on dress-making. The marketing side is really important and a key feature involves going to any exhibitions – such as wedding fairs – where I can meet people and get my name known. The downside? Doing the books.
>
> Jenny

'So how did these people change career? What's their secret? What sort of skills do you need to do it, and what do you have to find out?'

The individuals in this chapter identified what was important to them, and what interested them, and then focused their attention on creating a career out of it. Many other things in their lives had been put to one side while they achieved their goal. Changing career involves a process or a journey, for which you need to gather information, even if your gut instinct tells you it is right. So what information will you need to be confident you are doing the right thing?

1. *The 'how to do it' side.* This book will show you.
2. *Information on you* – yourself, your family and friends, past experience of life, experience of others, performance reviews at work, personal leanings.
3. *Information on careers themselves.* The Internet, careers books, employers, professional bodies, training organizations, education establishments, local authorities, the press, getting first-hand experience... all available at Internet cafes, public libraries, bookshops, airports, and careers events.
4. *Your own heartfelt reactions* – to what you are learning about yourself and what you want; and what is possible.
5. *Your circumstances* – how your proposed career change measures up to reality.

You will need the following skills to change career and ensure you are constantly employed, and this book will help you develop them:

- Assessing yourself: working out where you have got to in your working life and acknowledging the need to change.
- Understanding the workplace: what's going on there and how that is affecting employment opportunities, and especially working out the implications for you.
- Research skills: finding out about yourself and the workplace.
- Decision making: knowing how to make a well-informed career decision.
- Strategic management: having a vision and developing a strategy to carry it through.
- Taking responsibility for your own development and learning: organizing it so that you get to where you want to be.
- Self-marketing and promotion: landing yourself work, and knowing how the sectors you want to work in recruit people.
- Coping with change: handling stress and change.
- Interpersonal skills: relating to other people throughout the process.
- Self-management: coping and excelling at work and balancing life and achieving your goals.

Why work at all?

Let us examine the reasons why you want and need to work. The 20th-century American psychologist, Maslow, believed there were five levels of need. Most people must work to meet the first level, but after that, individuals have their own values and requirements of life.

Maslow's hierarchy of needs

Level 1	Physiological	Ensuring the basic needs of life: shelter, food, clothing
Level 2	Security	Meeting a need for routine and familiarity
Level 3	Affiliation	Gaining trust and acceptance
Level 4	Self-esteem	Feeling useful and needed; enjoying self-respect
Level 5	Self actualization	Realizing our potential through our values and beliefs

Do you go out to work solely to provide a roof over your head, food in your belly, and something to wear? Most people's lifestyles demand a salary that will provide them with far more than that, although there is usually more to work than just the financial benefits. Even those who win the Lotto often continue working. Some people need the routine and discipline of work to shape their lives, and the companionship of their colleagues. So what is it about work which makes people do it, even when they don't have to? The values in the bar below explain why people go out to work for more reasons than to meet Maslow's level 1 needs:

for a sense of achievement	for the power
belief in the job for its own sake	to be a professional
belief in the goals of the organization	to prove something to themselves or others
to belong somewhere	for the recognition
for the challenge	to have a routine in their life
to use creativity	for status in company/community
to be the expert everyone refers to	for the adrenaline buzz
because it is fun	the promise of training
to help others	to feel valued and needed
for their own self-identity	to win
to make a difference and contribute	because it is worth while
to reach their potential	to influence others
to meet the bills	to make lots of money
to build something successful	to take risks
to be independent	to get out of the house
to meet people	other

ASK YOURSELF

What do I value in a career or a job?

Looking at the above values, pick out the four most important to you. Rank them. Discuss them with somebody close you trust. What does that person think? Listen to his or her perspective – he or she might come up with a new point of view. Those values that you rate highly will feature strongly in your next career and influence the range of careers you consider. For example, they will help you determine whether you want a career or a job.

What does the word 'career' mean to you? According to the *Oxford Thesaurus*, it can mean employment, occupation, calling, vocation, pursuit, (life's) work, job, business, livelihood, profession, trade, craft or metier. Overall, these are careers that you would train for and work at. But your values for this career change may suggest that you just want a job, more likely designed to pay the necessary bills and give you the time you want to do other things that are important to you. Of course, a job can develop into a career, and, if you don't put the required effort into building it and look after it, a career can rapidly turn into just another old job.

NEXT STEP

What you value most from work will form a major cornerstone of your next career, so be sure of what you want.
Reflect thoroughly on what you value most from working. Talk to people you know who are really happy in their careers. What do they value most about them? Why did they choose them? Identify whether you want a career, which will need work and drive to get into; or just a job to pay the bills.

The reasons you work will impact on your thoughts about your future career, but they won't necessarily sit well with your ideal lifestyle and cherished material benefits. If you find a career that

31

gives you tremendous satisfaction but doesn't pay so well, then you will need to compromise.

Summary

- Learn from the efforts of other individuals.
- Be inspired.
- Develop a philosophy: think lifelong learning.
- Embrace change as a positive force.
- *Expect* to change career.

Summary exercises

1. Who do you know who has changed their career, or the way they work? Tell them you are contemplating a career change and ask them:

   - how they went about their change;
   - what made them change;
   - how the change has affected the way they and their family live;
   - what advice they have for people who are considering making a change as well?

2. Take three role models you admire and deem to be successful.

   - What makes them successful in your eyes?
   - How did they get to where they wanted to be?
   - How would you like to emulate their success?
   - What were the tactics/strategies they used to achieve their goals?
   - What has this taught you about what success means to you?
   - What can you learn from their motivation?

3. Look at the job you liked the best in your career, whether it was full or part time, or unpaid. What would you pack in a suitcase from each past job to take with you?

3 What is going on that makes it possible to change career?

Career paths do not exist any more

Career paths have been thrown upside down. The old certainties attached to a career have been blown away in a storm of change which shows no sign of blowing itself out. There are still professions with a fixed, structured and regulated programme of training and study, and practical experience to be undertaken before you are officially qualified. But as the competition for employees in many areas gets tougher, many professions have sought to widen the route 'in' for mature entrants. A career for life will be harder to find, which is why the trained-on-the-job employee who had hoped to stay in a job all their life, will find it harder to refocus and retrain. A life history is likely to be decorated with periods of the following:

- employment;
- unemployment;
- underemployment;
- retraining;
- study;
- time out;
- travel;
- maternity/paternity leave;
- temping;
- freelance work;
- contract work;
- casual labour;
- work abroad.

To cope with all these choices, you will need to have a strong sense of:

- self-worth: able to provide a rapid assessment of what you have achieved and what you can do, and want to do in the future;
- self-reliance: to rely on your own ability and decisions;
- a flexible approach, and an ability to spot and be ready to exploit opportunities;
- constant reappraisal of where you are and where you want to be – a sort of annual MOT of life;
- career and life-decision-making skills, as outlined in the previous chapter;
- change – an ability to cope with current and future changes;
- learning – to keep up to date with trends and new products;
- the importance of transferable skills and the ability to serve and care for others – a liking and an ability to work with people will be a key feature to the workplace;
- an understanding of how information technology can help you in managing your career and securing employment.

You will need to exercise all these features to remain in work that interests and motivates you throughout your career. The only way to guarantee a meaningful life over which you are in control will be to maintain a programme of lifelong learning and continual investment in new skills. Only then will you be in a position to take advantage of the opportunities life throws at you – even if you are in your 70s. As you work through this chapter, consider the ways in which you want to work in the future.

Employment patterns and ways to work are continually changing

As explorers, scientists, artists, religious leaders and inventors have done over the centuries, we have individuals who take courage in both hands and create change by pushing back boundaries and taking risks. In particular, we see young professionals who have made it before their mid-30s in a career that they didn't necessarily enjoy that much, but who have done well out of it and now want to do something more interesting and perhaps of greater value to society at large. These small businesses do not need to have success on such a scale as Anita Roddick or Richard Branson to drive change. They can do very nicely, thank you, in their local area if they spot a need for a new service. We live in a 'can do' society: individuals from any background can create change if sufficiently motivated to do so.

There has been a huge rise in demand for business and personal services

Many people are switching career to run their own businesses and offer services and products to those of us who want to make the most of our resources, especially time. Small businesses, freelancers and franchise operators are all benefiting from companies' and individuals' attempts to save themselves time and money and to cope with the pressures and stresses that the modern workplace brings. The pressure to perform over long hours for instance has created new careers looking after pets; animal behaviourists and pet therapists are seeing many pets whose owners are away from home for too long a period and causing their animals stress. The demand for business and personal services has led to an enormous number of opportunities for consultants, financial advisers, life coaches and executive coaches. Businesses taking tasks off other people leaving them free to focus on core activities are in demand. Increasingly, busy people are paying lifestyle managers and companies to take the hassle off their hands and out of their lives. Thus you could have a business organizing children's parties or weddings, landscaping gardens, doing ironing and cleaning, shopping and child/nanny sitting and dog walking. You don't necessarily have to do the tasks yourself: you can employ others to do the hands-on work, while you look after the direction of the business. Alternatively, you may be happy to do the nitty-gritty tasks yourself. Individuals with a flair for marketing and organizing have a plethora of niches to tap into, depending on their interests and own unique skills. Quality, personal service, and products with individual appeal are particularly essential components to any successful small business.

Ways to work have changed

The technology and communications revolution

The technology and communications revolution provided for a huge range of jobs. The good news for the person seeking to change career is that many employers want to recruit people with experience in other areas of business, and particularly social skills, the ability to handle people at all levels, business development, problem solving and team-working. Yes, an aptitude for working with computers is important, but then so is business awareness and customer service experience. The industry has also created a huge demand for trainers to run the vast number of courses now on offer to those seeking a career in the industry. The explosion of the Internet has enabled employment opportunities to come right into the home and the fortunes of small businesses have been transformed as the Internet has become their lifeline, offering career opportunities to people any-where. There are, for example, companies who will pay you to surf the Web, something easily done from home.

The technology and communications revolution has produced the 'I can work anywhere' approach, with companies and indi-viduals working from home or tele-centres (visit www.tca.org.uk – Web site to the Telework Association), which offers the advantage of sharing multimedia centres and facilities – even secretaries. These opportunities pose more issues for the person considering a career change. For example, would you be happy working in isolation at home, discussing work with the cat, or do you prefer to have your colleagues around you to grab a coffee when brainstorming a new service for your customers?

An important consideration in any change of job is thinking more carefully about the sort of team and organizational set-up you are looking for and the culture you want to join.

ASK YOURSELF
What sort of working set-up would I prefer?

Would you be happy:

- In a virtual office, where the team you are with links up weekly by conference call or video conference link, and otherwise contacts each other through e-mail and telephone, only meeting occasionally?
- Working at the first free desk you see every day, collecting your belongings from a locker at the start of the day?
- Working from your mobile phone, car and lap top?
- Going home at night knowing that 'your chair, your desk and your office' will still be there in the morning, along with the picture of your labrador, wife and children on your desk?
- To be outside virtually all day (including winter)?
- To be travelling as you're working (for example, as a travel courier or airline pilot)?

The work–life balance has become more important to many people

A further important feature of modern-day living is the quest for a better balance of life and work. People don't want to spend such a huge proportion of their lives working. They want their own private personal space to enjoy their hobbies, to do voluntary work and to uphold family commitments. Demographic and social trends are partly behind this desire for more flexible hours, as many of us have elderly relatives to care for, while dual-career and single-parent families have brought about a huge demand for childcare services.

Individuals are gaining confidence in asking for hours that suit them. This benefits employers, who don't need all of their staff all of the time and who want to cut costs to be competitive. Flexible working patterns enable us to work shifts, term time only, part-time, or a specified number of hours per annum when things are buzzing, and to enjoy sabbaticals and career breaks. Graham, an architect, retired by working increasingly less hours on a basis agreed with the other partners in the firm. He went half time for two years, then quarter time; then became a consultant. The money kept rolling in, he could build up a new life for himself and he didn't feel as if his world had suddenly come to an end.

Changes in working patterns

Thanks to customer demand for 24-hour service, there are far more part-time and temporary jobs about, and employee rights in these areas have gained ground as a result of new legislation. Your lifestyle could change dramatically if you restructure the hours you wish to work.

This could be useful as you prepare to change career, because if you can afford it, it may mean you can free up some time to gain valuable experience in your new line of work.

ASK YOURSELF

What sort of work–life balance do I want?

- How much of a work–life balance are you enjoying at the moment?
- Do you know anybody who seems to have it just right in your eyes? If so, how has he or she achieved what he/she wanted?
- How do your family and friends feel about the amount of time you spend working (including getting ready for work and making the journey there)?
- Which is more important to you: work–life balance, the lifestyle you want, or the career you want? How far are you prepared to compromise to get the best of everything?

NEXT STEP

**Work out whether you want the balance to be
different in the future.**

- If you have a partner, talk to him/her to see what he or she
thinks. He or she might want to have a change as well in
work–life balance.
- Visit the Work–Life Balance Team at www.dti.gov.uk/work-
lifebalance for some inspiration, news and views.

The way in which people are employed has changed

Efforts to enable companies to cope with a rapidly changing world
and respond to customer demands have resulted in flatter management structures and a change in the way companies employ people.
In *The Age of Unreason* (Arrow 1995), Charles Handy broke
employees down into three distinct groups.

- core workers: the professionals, technicians, managers,
central to the success of the organization, with skills and
organizational knowledge that is specific to the company;
- non-core employees, who do the non-essential work, who
have a good range of skills;
- flexible workers, the part-timer or temp whose hours can be
increased or decreased as required.

This is especially the case in industries such as leisure, hotel and
catering, and retail, where short term and part-time employment
opportunities have given companies the power to keep stores open
for longer, as demanded by customers, and employees the chance to
acquire working hours that are better suited to their individual needs.

These employment trends have been particularly welcomed by
the skilled individuals in society, who have seized the opportunity
to acquire greater job satisfaction, more flexibility and greater
control in their lives. People want the freedom to do their own thing
and many of those know that their expertise will enable them to

work for several different firms as opposed to one. This is the case with many of the people mentioned above.

Companies and organizations are outsourcing many areas: IT, payroll, training, building services, facilities management, catering, proof-readers, copy editors, marketing, sales and distribution, public relations, event organizers and personal service providers are all areas in which companies are using self-employed freelancers, which provides a wealth of opportunities for those seeking a career change. Teachers, health professionals, engineers, careers advisers, nursing and care staff all have the opportunity to start up their own businesses, working on a freelance basis, for example. There are plenty of opportunities through franchise operations meeting a wide range of interests, from catering to time management.

ASK YOURSELF

How closely do I want to be part of a business?

With regard to your lifestyle preferences, needs and values, which way would you prefer to work?

- as a 'permanent', core member of staff;
- as a 'temp' – these days, temps work in a wide range of sectors, and they are as likely to handle short-term projects and contracts as they are to cover for those on holiday or off sick;
- on a short-term or fixed-term contract;
- as an interim manager – a senior executive brought in to execute a specific project, bringing experience, a non-political approach and the ability to hit the ground running;
- as a consultant, brought in to bring a fresh point of view and a particular expertise, such as human resources or public relations;
- as a portfolio worker, with two or more part-time jobs;
- as a contractor or subcontractor.

Some sectors offer greater flexibility than others, but the search to recruit the best person for the task in hand and maximize resources has forced many employers to think creatively about the way they employ people. Check out www.flexibility.co.uk, a business newsletter published by the Home Office Partnership, which offers strategies and solutions for new ways of working; www.freelancecentre.com offers practical advice for those seeking to go freelance.

'I'm stressed! Help!'

The pressure on people to perform and exceed what is expected of them in a tough, unrepentant environment, has led to a rise in opportunities in the stress industry, as individuals try to find their own way to handle stress arising from life. The rise of alternative medicine as a complementary branch to the traditional ones has given rise to careers, such as homeopaths and herbalists, aromatherapists and reflexologists. People are also seeking ways to acquire fast ways to feel pampered and acquire a greater feeling of relaxation, which has led to a surge in new businesses such as nail clinics. The desire to push the body to maximum performance has led to new opportunities in fitness training, slimming, dress sense, and make-up artists.

ASK YOURSELF

Am I looking for a career with
less stress and pressure?

Some people thrive on adrenaline, others reach a point where they have had enough. Many high fliers reach a point when they suddenly say, 'That's it. I've had enough. Time to get off the treadmill and out of the rat race and enjoy life, instead of building up massive sums in the bank I never have time to enjoy.' In changing your career, ask yourself whether you are hoping to avoid stress and pressure in your next job – or whether you would get bored without that adrenaline rush.

Top Tip

Don't change career because you think you will get
an easier ride in another job or career.
Change because it means something to you.

Individuals are asking themselves what they have to lose

As we get older and the years pass by, people are less inclined to
waste time doing things they don't want to do and maturity gives us
the confidence to say so. The challenge in switching career is to find
work we enjoy and are good at, which makes us feel good about
ourselves and fits in with our values.

Look at this list of people who've moved out of the jobs on the
left, and into the jobs on the right:

bank teller	⇨	hairdresser
nurse	⇨	journalist
retailer	⇨	school assistant
hotel manager	⇨	training officer
teacher	⇨	bank manager
teacher	⇨	trainer
nurse	⇨	teacher
physiotherapist	⇨	teacher
social worker	⇨	animal welfare officer
company administrator	⇨	portfolio worker
presentation operator	⇨	pet-shop owner
secretary	⇨	fancy-dress shop manager
investment banker	⇨	painter
plumber	⇨	doctor
bank manager	⇨	vicar
secretary	⇨	journalist
insurance clerk	⇨	chef, patisserie
doctor	⇨	taxi driver

What can you say about these career moves? In many cases, individuals switched to jobs that:

- gave them a sense of autonomy and independence;
- gave them greater freedom of expression, and the opportunity to use their creative skills on the job;
- meant they had more fun at work;
- enabled them to make an intimate difference to the lives of others;
- gave them a different level of responsibility – more of it, or less;
- took them out of the larger, impersonal corporate organizations where they might easily feel unappreciated and moved to work in smaller working groups, eg for themselves or small companies and family firms;
- gave them more control over their lives and more influence over the direction of the way a business went;
- often meant they left jobs traditionally sold by careers services, schools and parents as 'secure, life long, respectable jobs with a pension at the end';
- required retraining to move into new areas, such as studying for an MBA funded by redundancy money; or training on the job under the NVQ system;
- enable them to fulfil their potential.

ASK YOURSELF
What am I looking for in a new career and a new employer?

Oh, the benefits of ageing!

Maturity gives you a better knowledge of who you are, what you like, what you care about, and a wider network of people you can turn to for help. And the good news is that there are employers who want and need maturity, plus some professions have fast-track routes for people changing career. People with experience of life and another sector bring expertise and examples of what has worked and what has not. In particular, charity organizations have been forced to develop a far more businesslike approach, with charity workers welcomed from other areas of life in fund-raising and volunteer management. When seeking work, you must be able to demonstrate to prospective customers, clients, and employers, how your past experiences and skills will benefit them.

The person moving to another career may bring good social skills, which is particularly important if they are to work with customers and clients of all backgrounds and ages. Voluntary interests can provide proof of an ability to handle a wide variety of people and form fast relationships with them, key skills in the workplace. If they are to be done well, many careers particularly require experience of life as customers prefer to deal with staff with maturity who have had experience of life and handling family matters. People with experience of life know all about the highs and lows, the struggles and joys, the worry and lack of confidence; they've been there. This is why the public and community sectors tend to welcome people seeking a career change. For similar reasons, some retail stores like B&Q recruit mature staff on the basis that they will have had their fair share of DIY. Others, such as Asda, appreciate that older staff help to portray the family atmosphere they seek to offer to customers. Many dot-coms seek to recruit people with experience of business life on the basis that clients feel better assured if there is somebody who can guide the younger, less experienced staff. They recognize the value of having a mixture of young and older staff as they balance out and provide the right sort of mixture of freshness and experience. When you are looking for prospective employers to work for, or starting your own business, think about the sort of image that that organization seeks to portray.

Careers that are ideal for the person who has done something else first and acquired experience of life include:

alternative medicine	charity work
animal care	the church
beauty therapy	some craft areas
careers advisory work	environmental health

driving instructor	management
financial advisory	media
services	museum work
funeral services	personal services
health care	police work
health and safety	probation work
horticulture	psychology
house sitting	retail
hotel management	security services
IT	social services
insurance	sports coaching
introductory services	teaching
legal services	teaching English
libraries	training
life coaching	working with children
local government	working with the elderly

Careers with a high degree of responsibility, such as company secretary, mean that maturity can be a tremendous advantage. Finally, attributes such as reliability, and a well-rounded work ethic, usually characteristic of those with experience of work, are very much appreciated by employers.

ASK YOURSELF

How could my background be of interest to an employer in a totally different sector?

- Of all the jobs listed above, pick the one which most appeals to you right now.
- Can you think of specific examples when you have been able to draw on past experience in your life to help you in your current role? Use your experience in its broadest sense.

NEXT STEP

Build your belief that you have something to offer other careers in terms of the skills and knowledge you have already.

Key skills transfer between jobs

I mentioned in the Preface that 'The Workplace' was like a huge jigsaw puzzle, with all the pieces linked together in some way. Transferable skills exist in every piece of the jigsaw, since every sector and each role within each sector needs them. They are so called because they will 'transfer' from one career to another. Their importance to the workplace has been reflected in the development of vocational qualifications such as GNVQs, Life Skills, Key Skills and NVQs. Examples include:

- communication;
- numeracy;
- IT;
- teamwork;
- flexible approach;
- motivation;
- enthusiasm;
- a proactive approach;
- business acumen;
- commitment;
- problem solving;
- managing your own learning and continuous development;
- customer care;
- building client relationships;
- networking;
- presenting;
- time management;
- planning and organizing;
- using your initiative;
- managing your workload.

ASK YOURSELF

What transferable skills do I have?

1. Consider the job you are doing at the moment, or the job you did most recently. Looking down that list of transferable skills, can you identify examples of times you needed to use those skills?
2. Now consider a job a friend is doing. Ask him or her to do the same exercise.
3. Compare notes as to how you used these skills and how much you both use the same sort of skill.
4. Where do your jobs differ in terms of the skills you use?

If you are going to change career, you will need to work out ways to show how your skills transfer from one sector to another, giving concrete examples and demonstrating how you would use them preferably in a culture and language your prospective employer can understand.

NEXT STEP

Transferable skills will go a long way to help you change career, but you'll need to do some training and/or learning.

To change career, you'll need to adapt to a new culture and environment. You will need to acquire new knowledge and language relevant to your new role by studying, training and talking to people working in it. What changes from one career to another is the *job specific* skills, ie the skills you need to do the particular job you have chosen to do. If you are a professional person used to reading around your area and picking up information at a rapid pace, this may be easier. If you are not, you may find it harder to achieve that focus. If you are going to read about things that naturally interest you, keeping up with trends and developments will be easier.

You can study full-time and part-time courses, distance-learning, modular courses taken bit by bit as and when you can fit them in – the ways to train have increased substantially.

To give you an idea of the range of subjects that can be studied, look at the list below. Bodies such as the City & Guilds provide a wide range of qualifications, which can be attained through a combination of practical experience and theoretical knowledge. Many of these courses can be studied on a distance-learning basis, with special provision being made for the practical side.

accounting	horticulture
agriculture	inn-keeping
animal care	insurance
aromatherapy	interior decorating
art and design	journalism
banking	legal studies
body massage	management
business administration	marketing
civil engineering	media studies
computing	multi-media
counselling	nursery nursing
creative writing	picture framing
credit management	public relations
customer care	quality assurance
debt recovery	social work
desktop publishing	sports coaching
electrical installation	teaching adult education
financial services	teaching English
food preparation	tour operator's certificate
health and holistic therapies	Web design
health-care	word processing

There are also a large number of one-year postgraduate courses which will prepare you for specific careers such as recreational management, law, teaching, and hotel and catering management. Visit www.prospects.ac.uk or www.hobsons.co.uk for more information on these, and on funding them.

The area of education and training, both on an individual and company level, has changed dramatically in an attempt to meet the demand for IT, vocational, technical and management programmes as multifunctional workforces become essential. There has been a tremendous expansion in jobs within the training sector, especially to help people develop skills, such as trainers, adult education, personal development, information management, library staff, Internet, teaching English as a foreign language, life coaching – even driving instructors. Some of these provide rapid routes into new careers, such as the government's fast track scheme for people seeking to train as teachers, while initiatives such as New Deal have created opportunities for individuals to take part in employment-based training. See www.newdeal.gov.uk.

Believe that change is possible – you can make things happen

At the very heart of the success of career changers is their belief that it is possible to change career. You need to believe this yourself, and recognize that it will take effort to achieve it. Chapter 2 showed you that yes, individuals are succeeding in changing career; and this chapter has showed you how opportunities to change are increasing. Harness that belief and a willingness to learn new tricks of the trade (or profession) to use in your working life, and you are on your way. If you want to change career, you will do it.

So boost your morale. Start telling yourself:

'Life's too short to be miserable at work. I can do something else.'
'If I'm going to have to work hard, I might as well do something I enjoy.'
'I want to have the energy to do something after work, not just slop in front of the telly and fall asleep, which I do at the moment.'
'I want the best life I can get. You only have one, after all.'

Summary

As a result of the changes that will continue to change the way we work, throughout your working life, you will need to think about the way you wish to live your life in terms of:

- career choices: what you want to do and how you want to work;
- financial planning: including provision for your own pension, insurance, budgeting;
- life management: handling relationships through a changing world, managing time and stress.

Summary exercises: sharpen your awareness of change

1. Do you consider yourself to be a driver of change? How can you demonstrate your answer?
2. Do you welcome change, or do you find it hard to cope with?
3. In your current job:

   - How have the changes mentioned above impacted on the organization you work for? And your job?
   - How has your job changed over the past two years or since you started?
   - How has it affected your boss's job?
   - How much of this change have you personally: 1) thought of; 2) planned; and 3) carried out?

4. Get hold of a copy of your local paper.

  - What sorts of changes have taken place?
  - How might these affect employment in the area?
  - What sorts of opportunities might they have provided for somebody looking to change career or start up a new business?

4 *Taking stock of what you want to do*

This chapter will ask you many questions about yourself so that you can find the work that suits you best. However, self-assessment is often the hardest part of career decision making and the bit people are most likely to skip over the most. Take plenty of time to answer the questions in this chapter, and to write down and mull over your thoughts. The interests, skills and qualities listed are merely examples, and not an exclusive list. I'm sure you will think of more. As you note down the things that interest you, try to pinpoint where in the workplace you could find them.

As you work through the next two chapters:

Start linking the broad elements you want in your new career to the sectors of work where they can be found.

Then research the range of opportunities within those sectors.

Come to a shortlist of careers that seem to match what you're looking for.

Within any given job, there are particular elements:

- the calling or motivation to do it;
- the people you want to work with – your colleagues, customers and clients;
- the way in which you know you've done a good job;
- the job-related skills you'll use (on top of transferable skills);
- the knowledge you'll use and keep up to date with;
- the qualities you'll need on the job;
- the level of training you'll need to get in there;
- how you would like to be rewarded, for example massive salary, flexitime, an outstanding reputation, a high status in the organization or community;
- how you'll want to be employed.

This chapter will take you through these and help you work out careers or opportunities that might meet your needs. You're looking for something that will make you tick and give your all; that will make you feel proud, satisfied and fulfilled; and that will give you the income you need to enjoy the lifestyle you want.

Dig deep to work out what makes you tick the most

Look to the past for clues as to what makes you tick and feel passionate. Think of tasks you have had to do within a job. Include your hobbies, interests and home activities such as DIY. Think about the involvement you have had with voluntary organizations, community work, local politics, educational establishments, cultural and spiritual activities. Use past performance reviews to identify your areas of strength and things you have achieved and enjoyed doing. Include anything you have initiated, and look back for flashes of inspiration you had to make the world a better place.

Go back to your childhood and example ideas and dreams that appealed to you then, before people told you to be more realistic, and suppressed your ideas because they weren't normal or safe enough. Think of what your ideal would be as you work through the chapter. Consider, for example, 'My gut instinct tells me ...' and 'My dream job is ...'.

As you look back, note all those things that drew out the best in you, and that you:

- enjoyed;
- did well at and were proud of;
- achieved;
- felt passionate about and interested in;
- contributed to;
- felt was natural and where you belonged;
- valued most;
- handled well.

Use them, plus your gut instinct and intuition, to do the exercises in this chapter and really dig deep to find out what makes you tick. Ask friends to help you on this journey. They know what enthuses you.

ASK YOURSELF

Am I veering towards any particular career?

Often, those of us wishing to change career will have nurtured a secret desire to do a particular job for a long time. You may have held secret aspirations that you never shared with anyone else, perhaps because you never dared to think you would achieve them; or perhaps your aspirations were so far removed from what family and school considered to be 'normal'. Fear of scorn from others, particularly about something so close to one's heart, can stamp out ideas faster than anything else. This is the perfect time for you to revive any secret dreams or aspirations you had concerning your career, and to see if you can make them come true.

If you have a secret dream career, here is a check list of things to ask yourself to prove that you are serious about it.

1. What is pulling you towards this idea?
2. How much do you know about the particular job?
3. Why do you think you would enjoy it?
4. How would it be valuable or important to you?
5. How long have you thought about this idea? Is it a recent whim, or have you harboured the thoughts for a long time?
6. How did you feel about it when you first thought about it?
7. How could you make this sort of work happen? How could you turn this idea into reality?
8. Would you still do it if you won the Lotto?

If your answers are making you sit up and feel excited, research your dream to see what it really involves. (Chapter 5 will show you how.) Could you make it a reality? It could be closer than you think!

What motivates you at work?

Aristotle said if an individual could work out where their talents and the needs of the world cross, there lies that individual's vocation. We all excel and enjoy things we are interested in and are good at, believe in and feel sufficiently strongly enough to do something about. Look at the box below (adding more if you think of other examples) and highlight those actions you would like to incorporate in your job.

advise others	help people with problems
turn something or someone around	bring order out of chaos
contribute to a cause or belief	develop an organization
motivate others to reach their potential	create things
have fun	build a business empire
bring out the truth	influence the direction of something

gamble and take risks	have the freedom to express myself
lead others	serve the community or your country
look after the welfare of people	uphold the law and rights
interpret the past and/or future	influence others
produce new products	help people make the most of their resources
help people reach their dreams, goals or aspirations	root out stories or the truth
design something	invent something
pull something together to make it happen	root out what is behind certain problems
develop technology	test things out
sell my expertise to others	make a difference
conserve something	other

For each action you highlight, build up a picture of how you might incorporate it at work. You could be using these actions at the moment in your current role, but may feel it is time to direct them to work in an area demanding different knowledge and where you will meet a new group of people. The exercises in this chapter will help you add to this picture. For example, if you want 'to help people with problems' build up a picture of the kind of groups of people you want to help, and the problems they might have. They might be in difficulties over debt, legal matters, housing, health, employment needs or personal issues. Whatever area of their lives you choose to help them with, you will need to have a natural interest in reading and learning about it, so that you can keep up to date with trends and developments, such as legislation and government policies, so it is important to zoom in on what excites, touches and interests you because you will be using that knowledge at work. You might need to be firm with people and patient if they have difficulty understanding what you are telling them.

ASK YOURSELF

Who do I want to work with? Who do I want my colleagues and customers or clients to be?

As most careers involve working with people, you are more likely to find the right role by tapping into the sorts of colleagues, customers and client groups you most want to work with. Which groups of people do you want your job to bring you into contact with most, or who do you want to make a difference to? With which group do you identify best of all, empathize with most easily and feel most comfortable? Highlight any groups in the box below which really reach out and touch or excite you.

different nationalities	the unemployed
locals	politicians
people with relationship difficulties	people without hope
criminals	organizations as a whole
leaders	the disabled
children	people with learning difficulties
babies	the bereaved
teenagers	students
the elderly	tourists

parents/parents to be	animals
professionals in other sectors	the general public
professionals in the same field	adults seeking work
colleagues only	service providers
business clients	creative people
other	

What has life taught you about working with those groups you have highlighted? Talk to people who work with them. What are the up- and down-sides? If you have been used to working with highly driven professionals, how would you cope if you were working with people who were barely articulate or had no ambition all day and every day?

ASK YOURSELF

How much do I want my new career
to mean that I interact with people?

How should that contact take place, and how often? If you want lots of contact with people using caring and creative skills, you could look at beauty therapy or alternative medicine. If, however, you want plenty of people-contact in a caring environment, but you're more interested in how the mind works, you could look at psychology.

So consider how much contact you want with people, and how you want it to take place:

- face to face;
- in a practical, hands-on way;
- over the phone;
- as little as possible – you've had enough of the human race.

If the last line sounds like you, you may prefer one of the following options:

- 'I prefer data to people – economics, statistics, history, science, information technology, mathematics, finance…'
- 'I prefer things to people – plants, buildings, water, air, the earth, energy, fabrics, colours, food…'
- 'I prefer ideas to people – stories, visual, business, political, religious beliefs, concepts…'

NEXT STEP

Start linking these ideas to the workplace.

'Where will I find those people, ideas and things I want to work with and help? How do I reach out to them?'

Brainstorm those places where you might meet and work with the people you feel most comfortable with, in terms of your future colleagues and then again with the groups who touch you the most. Get friends you trust to brainstorm with you over a glass or two of wine – there's nothing like it to get a great mind map going. If you wanted to reach out and work with people of all different nationalities, for instance, you might consider these choices (these are not exclusive, they are just examples):

- businesses: eg a global organization, such as an accountancy firm or bank;
- diplomatic service;
- international charities organizations, such as the Red Cross;
- visitors – eg tourist attraction, hotel, local tourist information centre, travel companies such as airlines;
- international political organizations such as the EU or NATO;

- welfare – eg immigration centre, charity;
- legal – eg customs officer, policeman on the street.

Then add more ideas by:

- checking the Yellow Pages;
- checking the newspapers' recruitment pages;
- visiting the Internet, and searching for Web sites with just your keyword;
- visiting your local library;
- reading the local press to get an idea on the 'things are happening' front;
- walking down your high street to see who operates there.

ASK YOURSELF
What do I want to achieve in my career?

We all view success and achievements differently. Which of the following outcomes would you consider to be the kind of success you would like to achieve at work, something that would tell you you had done an excellent job you could be proud of? If somebody gave a speech about you at your funeral, what would you want them to say you excelled at?

- exceeding targets;
- clinching the deal;
- influencing people;
- securing promotion;
- developing a motivated, successful team;
- helping someone through a sticky patch;
- developing an individual;
- seeing your idea come into being;
- acquiring a hefty bonus;
- having a positive influence on someone;

- getting good results;
- recognition for a job well done;
- financial rewards;
- acquisition of a company;
- inventing something;
- greater responsibility;
- influencing the direction of something;
- securing another contract as a result of what you have done;
- moving somebody forward in their thinking;
- offering a new service;
- happy customers;
- creating a new product;
- justice;
- deciding policies;
- happiness doing what you are doing;
- recommendations which are taken up;
- developing and implementing new strategies;
- a sale;
- a new structure such as a building, piece of furniture, item of clothing;
- setting up a new system;
- smooth day-to-day running of a business;
- seeing an idea turn into reality;
- a new look, eg Web page, fashion design, garden.

How you view success will depend on the way in which you can help people and make a difference. If you view targets and influencing the direction of something as success, and you wanted to help young people, you might enter the management levels of the local social or health services. You may get considerable satisfaction from seeing an overall reduction of teenage pregnancies in your area. Equally, you might want to help young people but see your way to measure success far more as the guidance you have given to one young life, to help them through a tricky patch. This ideal you have will also determine to an extent the sort of organization you work for – or whether you set up the business on your own.

ASK YOURSELF

What sort of an impact do I want to make?

It is possible for politicians to impact on the community, as a result of their work, and on the nation. Consider whether you prefer to work with the 'big picture' and strategy and the direction of something with an eye for detail, or more on a one-to-one basis, where you are helping an individual.

ASK YOURSELF

What job-related skills do I want to use at work?

What are you naturally good at doing? For example, there may be two people who have the same idea of what is important to them in their job – perhaps seeing justice done. But they may want to use different skills to get the job done. A policeman and a judge both want the same outcome, but they work to achieve it from different angles. The policeman seeks to investigate what really happened; the judge oversees cases brought to court and administers justice. Both, however, apply their knowledge of law to their work.

The Oxford Thesaurus provides other words for 'skills' as talent, ability, aptitude, expertness, expertise, facility, skilfulness, art, artistry, cleverness, adeptness, adroitness, mastery, dexterity, handiness, ingenuity, experience, proficiency, finesse, accomplishment, forte, strength, gift, capability, know-how. Using these words to help you, and the examples of skills listed below:

- Which skills do you enjoy using?
- Which skills are you interested in using, but feel you need to develop more?
- Which skills would you like to use at work for the majority of the day?

- Which skills would form a key part in your new career?

Examples of skills

addressing groups

advising

analysing

announcing

balancing the needs of the individual and the organization

coaching

controlling quality

coordinating

creating

debating

delivering results to a budget/deadline

designing

detecting

developing

examining

exercising judgement

explaining (complex) things clearly

feel for languages

fund raising

gathering information

handling large amounts of data

interpreting information

identifying

identifying salient points out of much data

imagining

implementing something

inspiring

judging cost effectiveness of something

juggling

leading groups

listening

making things

managing

marketing

measuring

monitoring

motivating

negotiating	relating to selling
nimble-fingered	stimulating others
observing	supervising
organizing	training
paying close attention to detail	translating
	trouble-shooting
persuading	understanding implications of actions
planning	
presenting	understanding laws and regulations
prioritizing	
programming	understanding the needs of others
promoting	using hands
public speaking	visualizing
recruiting	working under pressure
researching	writing

NEXT STEP

Think about ways in which you want to use the skills you've pinpointed at work. Try to describe the sort of place you see yourself doing them in. Skills can be used in different ways. For example, people who manage may have responsibility for people, information, systems, finance, the day to day running of an organization, events or facilities. Each is a career in its own right.

ASK YOURSELF

What sort of knowledge do I want to learn about and apply on the job?

Knowledge can transfer between careers (although you still have to keep updated with it), just as skills can. A mathematics and economics teacher, Paul switched career to go into operational research. His knowledge of maths and economics was essential to his new career, but there were certain skills he could leave behind (like having eyes in the back of his head) as he developed new ones (assembling and understanding information relating to a problem area). His communication skills as a teacher were crucial to doing his new job well.

Most people have a particular subject or knowledge they pick up more readily than others – it comes naturally to them and they have a natural aptitude for it. Think back to your school days. Which classes did you love and find easy? Science? Maths? Humanities? Sociological subjects? Which ones did you hate and always try to wrangle out of? These can point you to the sort of knowledge you might want to use in the job, and they may include:

- animals;
- arts;
- beauty;
- biology;
- calligraphy;
- chemistry;
- colours;
- crafts;
- design;
- earth-related;
- economic;
- education;
- electronics;
- employment;
- engineering;
- fashion;
- figures;
- film/theatre;
- finance;
- food/drinks;
- geography;
- hardware;
- health;
- health and safety;
- history;
- how the body works;
- how the mind works;
- information technology;

- Internet;
- languages;
- law and order;
- leisure;
- leisure attractions;
- materials;
- mathematics;
- mechanical;
- media;
- people – children, elderly, disabled, the public;
- photography;
- physics;
- plants;
- printing;
- psychology;
- risk;
- scientific;
- social/society;
- software;
- sport;
- standards;
- statistics;
- textiles;
- typography.

ASK YOURSELF

How central to my job do I want
my area of knowledge to be?

The way you want to use your knowledge and apply it can make a big difference to the range of career opportunities facing you. For example, if you loved languages, would you want to use them as a core part of your work, perhaps as a translator or interpreter, or as a complementary support, using them only when you speak to clients in their language? Think too about how much of a specific niche you want to develop. Do you want to be a specialist, and focus on a particular area, such as linking drug abuse to driving accidents, or a generalist, looking at what causes driving accidents generally?

NEXT STEP

**Relate the knowledge you want to use to sectors
of work.**

Traditional careers libraries operate a careers classification index dividing the workplace up into groups to facilitate the organization of materials. This may help you identify particular groupings of sectors you would like to work in. The index is organized as follows:

- self-employment;
- armed forces;
- administration, business, clerical and management;
- art and design;
- teaching and cultural activities;
- entertainment and leisure;
- hospitality, catering and other services;
- health and medical sciences;
- social and related sciences;
- law and related work;
- security and protective services;
- finance and related work;
- buying, selling and related services;
- sciences, mathematics and related work;
- engineering;
- manufacturing industries;
- construction and land services;
- animals, plants and the environment;
- transport.

If you visit any careers-related Web site, such as www.reed.co.uk, you'll see that such sites have their own groupings of the workplace, which are similar but may have more emphasis on newer careers. Check them out to get an overall view. It may help you clarify your thoughts as to where your career lies.

NEXT STEP

Which roles or specific careers need the knowledge and skills you want to use in your new career?
Examples are science for health and healthcare companies, or economics and maths for banking and risk management.

Look for sectors that would enable you to incorporate the things you want in a job and the opportunities which relate to your interests. If you want to serve the community, for example, think about the civil service, local government, and services such as law enforcement or local politics, health or education.

Knowledge goes out of date rapidly. To excel on the job (and enjoy it), you need to keep up with product development, trends, what competitors are doing, new advances and demands. Much of this will probably be done in your spare time. Frequently, professional bodies demand members take a specified period of 'continued professional development' (CPD) every year. If you find an area of knowledge that interests you and for which you have a natural aptitude, keeping up to date and meeting CPD requirements won't seem so hard.

Top Tip

Think about the training you'll be undertaking.
Examine the content of any courses you'll need to do.
Are all the subjects that you'll cover of interest to you?

ASK YOURSELF

Can I turn my hobby, my skills or a voluntary commitment I have into a career?

The activities you choose to do in your spare time provide powerful indicators for people seeking to switch career because you have chosen to do them. If you can identify skills and a specialist knowledge which you have acquired through a particular hobby, such as history or gardening, or through voluntary work such as helping disturbed teenagers, then you could have a new career on your doorstep. Hobbies and voluntary efforts both enable you to develop skills and enhance your knowledge through practical hands-on experience or even through a system of examinations and training. They can lead to a new career, either launching your own business or working for somebody else doing something you love. People with serious hobbies or voluntary commitments usually have an excellent network of contacts of people already, which is useful in determining business needs in the area and spotting opportunities and 'getting in' to a sector.

Additionally, you can pass your knowledge on to others by teaching 'your' subject at further education colleges or through the media, by writing books and articles, as a technical author. So you may be able to combine some of these interests with skills in more than one way. For example, if you are interested in calligraphy:

- set up a business doing calligraphy for dinner parties, etc;
- give talks about calligraphy;
- write articles;
- run an adult education class.

Hobbies may provide you with ideas of other careers related to your interests. Joanna loved horses, but she didn't like riding them, nor did she relish the idea of spending her working life mucking out and cleaning tack. She was creative and had business acumen, and she was practical and enjoyed turning ideas into reality. She joined a small company that made equestrian videos. She was constantly in touch with an interest – horses – but at a level which didn't require such a hands-on approach. Her knowledge of them, and interest, meant those requesting the videos were more inclined to trust her judgement. She still needed to use skills in marketing and spotting gaps in the market. Think of the organizations you use in relation to your hobbies and voluntary pursuits. Had you ever thought of working for them?

Could you make money from any of the skills you have, if you marry them with your interests? What gives you a buzz? For example, you love pulling things together to make things happen, why not organize conferences for companies, or weddings for couples, or children's parties, stag and hen nights? If you have got imagination, a creative flair and business acumen, and you are into design, why not get a new career in Web design?

'I think I can take my hobby full time. I think. How can I be sure it is the right thing to do? I've spotted gaps in the market where I've got something to offer.'

It is one thing to have a hobby for fun – and quite another to do it full time for economic survival. What you need to work out is:

- what sort of activities your business will offer;
- what you will charge;
- how much call there is for doing that sort of thing;
- what you would need to get started;
- how you would market yourself.

Look at adverts in the paper, check the Internet for career details on professional bodies' Web sites and do your homework. If income will be sporadic until you get going, supplement your income by working part time, so that you can devote either a couple of days a week or every other week to your goal.

ASK YOURSELF

What sort of qualities do I want to use at work?

People at work all have different qualities. Nurses need to be patient and kind, but firm, able to instil confidence in their patients. Consider the sorts of qualities you would like to use in the job. Work out which qualities come naturally to you and show a friend or partner your list. Do they agree, and are there any others they would like to add?

accurate	enthusiastic	pleasant
adaptable	fair	practical

aggressive	firm	proactive
ambitious	flexible	reassuring
approachable	good memory	reliable
assertive	helpful	resilient
authoritative	inquisitive	resourceful
calm	integrity	sense of humour
caring	kind	smart appearance
committed	methodical	sympathetic
demanding	neat	tactful
determined	non-judgemental	thoughtful
diplomatic	objective	tolerant
direct	patient	unflustered
discreet	performer	

ASK YOURSELF

What sort of day to day routine do I want?

- How much routine do you want in a job? Do you want every day to be pretty much the same, or prefer something where no two days are alike?
- How physical and practical do you want your new career to be?
- How much action do you want in a day; what sort of speed and pressure do you want to work under?

ASK YOURSELF

What sorts of checks and systems do I want to work
with? How much do I want my new career to be
bound by things I have to adhere to, such as:

- systems and procedures;
- bureaucracy;
- laws;
- professional regulations and standards;
- ethos;
- values;
- management layers (although they are flat-
  tening out, they still exist);
- the job description;
- autonomy or lack of it?

Some people find handling bureaucracy such a nightmare that they
don't want to see any of it in their new careers. Others are quite at
home handling it and accept that it comes with the territory. Think
about your personality. Are you the sort of person who gets
extremely irritated by systems, procedures and bureaucracy,
preferring the more creative approach, or do you happily work
along with them? Others may be frustrated at having to stick to a job
description, preferring to take on anything that comes their way.
Think about the sort of person you are, and how you handle any
restrictions on you.

ASK YOURSELF

How much training am I prepared
to do towards my new career?

Do you want to train for a specific career which will demand a certain and possibly structured period of training and practical experience before you qualify? Or are you more interested in working as a generalist?

Within most sectors, there will be a range of different careers for which the study of qualifications will either enhance your chances of landing work or be essential to qualify. In the sectors you have unearthed that would enable you to do work which matters to you for a group of people who touch you strongly, consider the range of opportunities that exist. Each sector will offer a range of employment opportunities like this:

- professional and management;
- associate professional/technician;
- secretarial/manual/clerical;
- own business.

ASK YOURSELF

What would I do to get the career I want?

---

1. How much training are you prepared and able to do to change career? How would you do this training, ie: full time/part time/distance learning/e-learning? How long for? A short course over a few weeks as an intensive course?
2. Would you want to train for a specific profession or job, such as a physiotherapist or interior designer, or simply move to an area where you can apply the skills and knowledge

you have acquired through your own open learning which doesn't require such a structured learning process?

3. What level of work do you want to attain and how would the training required for that level differ to other levels? How do the responsibilities and day-to-day, or week-to-week, work compare and how might those impact on the sort of lifestyle you want?

4. Aside from the knowledge based/vocational training, how many added value skills are you prepared to obtain? For example, would you be prepared to attended courses designed to boost your abilities and help you achieve your goals, such as 'Running your own business' or 'Boosting your Business with IT'?

5. How much continual professional development are you prepared to do after qualifying? Some professional bodies demand that members undertake a set number of hours every year.

6. If the career is really, really something you want to do, would you do the training whatever the cost?

Your enthusiasm to change to a particular career may mean you decide to sacrifice a certain sort of lifestyle.

What sort of lifestyle do you want?

Consider the way you want to live your life and what you want to do in it. The decision to switch career provides an opportunity to transform your lifestyle. A key feature in changing your career will be evaluating the lifestyle you want – or, perhaps, _expect_ to have after you have achieved that switch. Certain careers will bring a particular way of living and will determine, amongst other things, the location of your work, travel opportunities, the hours you do, the sort of things you want to enjoy out of work, the clothes you wear, the exotic holidays, private schooling for the children, a fashion-designer wardrobe, top of the range sports car. They may involve lengthy, pressurized hours. Do you want to be a high-flier – or do you want to get off the treadmill and have more time for other things? If you were to look back later in life, how would you want your life to look, both in and out of work? Much depends on what is happening in your own life now. If there are things that are important to you outside work, you may want more free time to do some of the things you love in your spare time – drama, music, writing, gardening. These things can enrich your life and bring you happiness and fulfilment in ways that no material benefits can as they provide for Maslow's fourth and fifth levels of needs, as outlined at the end of Chapter 2. If you want your lifestyle to continue in the same vein after you have changed career as it stands now, enjoying the same sorts of holidays, clothing and lifestyle, the range of opportunities open to you would be rather more limited than if you were prepared to draw in the purse strings and economize.

In the two columns below, which is the more important to you now, based on your experience of the workplace and your wishes for the lifestyle you want in the future?

high financial rewards	financial 'doing okay'
secure employment	constantly having to look for new work
live to work	work to live
a career	a job
to take work home with you	to lock up after work and turn off totally
work, work, work	work, hobbies, interests, fun
to be on call	not to be interrupted by the telephone from work when at home
to do shift work	have an idea of your hours
to have to fulfil a specific amount of professional training and development every year	to keep up to date because you want to
to commute	to work locally

| lots of stress | total reduction in stress element |
| to travel in the job | to stay put – visiting clients means you can be home in time for dinner |

Your reasons to work and the type of lifestyle to which you aspire will dictate to an extent the sort of job you will have later on. If you want to put 'oomph' into your career, you will need to devote hours of your free time doing that, by study or taking on projects over and above your responsibilities at work. If you want to run your own business or buy a franchise, it will probably be at least a couple of years before you start making a profit and, during that time, your spare time and holidays will possibly be severely curtailed. However, if it is taking you down the path to achieving what you want, then it is going to be worth it.

Would you want to give up a luxury lifestyle and the status of being a big fish in your company, if that is what your current job involves, especially if you have dedicated your life to get to where you are now and enjoyed little else along the way? When the message goes round that you are leaving, most of your colleagues will probably be thinking, 'Good for you – I'd do anything to do that.'

If you are really brave, you could downsize with the same company you are with now, as Barbara did:

It's very social working on reception. As an executive secretary, I was fed up of the long hours, being on call at weekends and never knowing when I was going to finish my working day. I didn't want to leave this firm, because I've got many friends here and the benefits are very good. So I changed my job. Now, I can arrive at nine, finish at five and have a full lunch hour. The drop in salary has been well worth it. I've got energy to do things I want to do which don't cost very much – like a course in English literature – and I know I can get away on time to my class, or meet friends. I've got my life back. People tell me I look 10 years younger. I certainly feel it.

Barbara

ASK YOURSELF

HOW DO I WANT TO WORK?

Do you want to be employed by somebody else? The benefits will include a regular pay check, holidays and, if you are lucky, a whole range of perks that the self-employed have to decide whether or not to take out on their own – health insurance, pension plan, etc. The downside is you have less control over your working life. This can all tie in strongly with the sort of lifestyle you want to lead.

Which of these appeal to you, bearing in mind your career and lifestyle ambitions?

regular pay check	irregular pay
set number of holidays	holidays depend on business
usually have weekends free	may have to work weekends and evenings, especially at first
work with a like-minded group of people	work solo
work to goals set by the company at their pace	work to achieve your own goals at your pace
achievements are shared with team	achievements are yours
you have little say (unless you are very senior) over the direction of the company	you are in the driving seat

you don't like risk	you are happy to take a gamble
you find it hard to identify gaps in the market	you have spotted a gap in the market for something you could offer

What are your answers telling you about the way you want to work? If they are telling you that, rather be employed by somebody else, you prefer to run your own business or buy a franchise, you will need to think carefully about how you would cope. Working from home, for example, isn't all it's cracked up to be:

I don't miss the daily commute – it takes me a few seconds to get to my office and that's free, too. But I do miss the team work and going out for drinks after work, or out for a pub lunch with my colleagues. I'm surprised at how much I missed it... the Monday morning chat over the coffee machine about the weekend. It is not the same over the telephone.

Sammy

If you are interested in running your own business, consider the following:

- Are you a driver and creator of change?
- Do you like taking risks?
- Are you prepared to commit yourself wholly to getting a business off the ground?
- Are you prepared to work long hours and have fewer holidays than you are used to, while you get things going?
- Can you work without supervision?
- How much support do you need at work?
- Could you buy a franchise?
- Do you have any start-up capital?

- Can you form good relationships with customers and clients and develop them?
- Have you got the skills you need to run your own business? For example:

– budgeting;	– recruiting;
– costing;	– creating;
– marketing;	– caring;
– negotiating;	– juggling several things
– organizing;	at once;
– networking;	– stickability;
– able to relate to people;	– an ability to know
– self-motivation;	when you need to seek
– decision making;	advice or help;
– administering;	– confidence.
– possibly supervising;	

If you have answered yes to most of these questions, then running your own business or going freelance may be for you.

Summary

1. Don't feel bound to choose your career at the level at which you are qualified, ie to go for a profession just because you have got a degree. There is no point if you would rather do something wild and 'wacky'.
2. Remember, be prepared to throw everything up in the air. The stuff which comes back down to earth to join you is telling you something. Stick with it.

Summary exercises

1. What have I learnt about myself and the career I am looking for so far?
2. Of these elements involved in a career and lifestyle (calling or motivation, the people I work with, the job-related skills,

knowledge and qualities I use, the level of training I will need, and the way in which I want to be employed), which to me are:

- essential;
- nice to have;
- not important;
- completely irrelevant?

3. Which sectors seem to match what I am looking for?

5 Linking you to the workplace – do your research!

If you've thought through the previous two chapters carefully, by now certain ideas should be coming to mind about possible new directions your career could take. The exercises in the previous chapter will have helped you build up a picture of the sort of role your're looking for within them.

NEXT STEP

Research the opportunities within the sector(s) which seem to meet your interests in terms of values and knowledge or the jobs that are beginning to appeal.

You can find out about the workplace by reading widely, surfing the Internet and talking to people. Research takes time, but it enables you to:

- broaden your range and knowledge of opportunities (note the word, opportunities, not jobs) in areas which interest you;
- prove to yourself that yes, you are heading in the right direction – you are shifting towards a vision of yourself in a particular area at work, and need to dig deeper to find where you will finally settle;
- expand your network of contacts;
- show those recruiting that you know what you are letting yourself in for and you will not be such a risk to take on;
- sell yourself more effectively throughout the entire process of changing career;
- boost your confidence and belief that you can do it.

This applies whether you are going to apply for a job as an employee, go freelance, or run your own business. This chapter will show you some of the organizations who can help you through all three avenues. In doing your research, three key things to note are:

1. Your information must be up to date and accurate, so go to professional bodies and organizations as opposed to relying on hearsay and friends' views.
2. While it is always worth talking to people actually doing the job, remember that their values and needs may be different to yours.
3. You will have far greater personal interest in digging for information than the person you are asking for help; so learn what you can from them and don't leave your quest for knowledge and detail at that: keep searching.

Get hard facts

The following groups offer three avenues to access information: printed materials, individuals and Internet Web sites:

- government education and employment departments;
- colleges, universities and training providers;
- recruitment agencies;
- financial service institutions;
- careers services;
- support bodies;
- management bodies;
- self-employed, freelancers, franchisees;
- professional bodies and trade associations;
- employers and employees;
- local governments;
- job centres;
- the media and press;
- private career services;
- small, medium and large employers.

Printed materials

Printed reading materials include such items as books, leaflets and videos, available in public libraries, careers libraries in universities, colleges and careers services, and bookshops. Traditional careers libraries operate a careers classification index to facilitate the organization of material as outlined in Chapter 4.

If your public library has a business reference section, you will find a lot of useful information, including sector reports. Many offer the facility of a business researcher, and they should all have details of local and national organizations, charities, committees and associations, not to mention books, journals, trade journals, newspapers, reports, developments, market and sector research reports and books listing companies. Add to this your usual careers library and you will see why your public library is worth a visit.

Individuals

Individuals are available who can help you make sense of the information, whether they work in the specific sector or in supporting agencies, or perhaps even people you know personally.

Internet Web sites

If you can visit sites with a fairly clear idea of what you want to find out, you are more likely to proceed through the huge amount of information more quickly and get the details you want. Be as specific as you can when entering the 'search' engines; simply putting the words 'careers' or 'jobs' will yield results of thousands of sites. Be prepared to route around Web sites to get the information you want, and be creative in thinking of things to search for – a change of word can do wonders for getting to the right Web site.

If you don't have access to the Internet, try your local careers service or library, and visit www.netcafeguide.com for a list of Internet cafes. Don't check out the Net using your computer at work: most employers will track any careers or job sites you visit. If you find a particular site of interest, it makes sense to Bookmark it to speed your return to it.

What can the Internet do for you?

The Internet is a huge mine of up-to-date information, so you will not be surprised to learn of at least two books you can refer to which have been devoted entirely to the subject. '*Surfing Your Career*' has over 1,500 Web sites, covering careers, job hunting, education and training. '*Net that job*' is particularly useful for an overview of how the Internet can help you find work. Some of the ways the Internet can provide you with information in order to help you decide on your future career are:

- giving you help on searching for that job, or contract (see Chapter 9);
- bringing into your home information on learning, retraining and educational opportunities;
- bringing into your home the opportunity to search for work anywhere in the world; as the Internet has a global reach, you can register with companies, recruitment agencies and sites established to help people find work, sending them copies of your CV and having access to banks of vacancies;
- enable you to check out what sorts of organizations recruit in an area and who is competing against whom;
- bringing a careers library straight into your own home;
- providing you with links to other useful Web sites to save your searching;
- it can save time, provided that you don't get distracted by other sites;
- it puts you in touch with your regional and national government to find out what initiatives they are taking to boost employment in your area, what they are doing to help people set up their own business or buy a franchise, or those seeking to retrain;
- it is generally kept well up to date;
- you can e-mail organizations and companies for information;
- it has search engines to help you find what you want;
- it can be particularly useful if you are looking for a niche area.

NEXT STEP

Find out about specific opportunities within the sectors that interest you.

The quickest way to get an idea for careers in a sector is to go to its professional body or trade organization. They lay down certain standards of education, training and continued professional development members must acquire in order to be recognized, practising members of the profession. They can provide:

- an overview of the industry;
- an idea of what careers are specific to it;
- profiles of individuals in different roles, so you can see what they would involve;
- details of courses and details of funding available (with search tools on Web pages to look for the course you want);
- links to other bodies who might be able to help you;
- advice for late entrants as to the best way 'in';
- discussion forums – why not e-mail to ask advice as to the best way in?
- advice for people with special needs;
- the future needs of the industry;
- placement opportunities;
- the qualifications required and length of training needed to qualify;
- recruitment services, often online;
- opportunities for working for yourself;
- opportunities for networking, such as via local and regional events;
- professional development and training courses;
- sometimes, lists of employers who are recruiting in your area;
- frequently asked questions – a list of questions from the public seeking more information.

Most professions have their own magazine, newspaper or publication; you can obtain details of these from the professional body itself or your newsagent. They may be in your local reference library, too. Magazines and publications enable you to: 1) learn about trends in the sector, what is happening, current issues and skills shortages; 2) refer to things you have read when you are talking to people in that sector – a sure sign of your interest; and 3) pick up useful tips relating to recruitment. Nor should you forget local branches of organizations such as the Institute of Management, and community service organizations such as Rotary, Lions, Round Table, Roteract and Soroptomists International, all of whom have a wide cross-section of members who may be willing to help further if you were to write. Citizens Advice Bureau offices should be able to put you in touch with club secretaries.

NEXT STEP

Try to get a feeling for the sectors that interest you:

- Who are the main players in this sector? What changes are they going through? What are the employment opportunities like?
- How competitive is it to get a job in this sector? (Don't be put off if the answer is, very.)
- How much and how far will you have to move about to be promoted (if that is what you want)?
- What are the normal working patterns? Is it a sector that relies heavily on contract workers, and if so, what are the more common contract periods?
- What is the pay going to be like immediately you start in your new career? And in three years' time?
- What are the strengths, challenges, weaknesses and threats facing people in this sector? What is being done by governments, organizations and individuals to meet them?

Professional bodies will introduce you to a range of opportunities within a sector. To get more details, you can search the Internet, international business reference books and the _Yellow Pages_ and press to build up a greater picture of the sorts of employers who operate in areas where your heart wants you to work. The Further Information sections at the back of this book will give you many addresses of professional and trade organizations.

'Where can I find out about the employers operating in the sector in which I want to work?'

Collectively, the Internet and *Yellow Pages* can provide you with a good picture of all the companies that operate in the sectors interesting you, and they can be very helpful if you are thinking of running a particular business and want to make sure that nobody else has thought of your idea in your area first. But you can also refer to your local library's reference section which should have other directories to help you find out which employers operate in your locality, while at the same time paying attention to the local press may also guide you to companies who may be able to help.

Large-, medium- and small-sized companies all have benefited enormously from the Web. It provides them with a global platform from which they can promote their products, services and job opportunities. From the huge global accountancy practice to the delicatessen in Scotland, the Internet has provided a voice. A company's Web site may outline its products, services, history, press releases, management teams (together with a brief history of their career backgrounds), and information for job seekers. Information about working for the company may appear under 'careers', 'recruitment', 'come and work for us', 'jobs' or 'human resources'. Some companies offer visitors a questionnaire to determine if you are right for them. If you come away feeling that you didn't press the right buttons, don't despair: it could be their image is not right for you. Their competitor might suit your needs and values more closely. When you visit a company's Web site or read any printed material, try to consider what sort of image the company is trying to portray and how that fits in with your values.

ASK YOURSELF

What sort of employer do I want to work for?

- What size employer do you want to work for? A large company may offer more chances of promotion, a small one the chance to get stuck in and more involved in decision making.
- Does its status matter to you? Do you want to work for a company that is a major name in its sector, and one everybody has heard about, a company that considers itself to be a leader? Or aren't you terribly worried about that; you feel you've left it all behind?
- What sort of work culture should the organization embrace? What sort of ethos and image should it portray?
- How much of a geographical reach should it have? International? National? Local?
- Should it be in the public/private/charity sectors?

The Internet gives you the chance to learn much more about a company from the comfort of your home at a far faster rate than ever before. For employers, it means they can reach a far wider audience. Look at the 'News' page or go outside the company's Web site and look for news releases and anything you can find about it. What sort of message is coming over? Is the company expanding? Is it into developing its staff? Is the Web site updated regularly? How much voice do the staff have on the site? Is there a chat room, for example? Initial impressions can tell a lot. How quickly do they respond to your e-mail request for information?

Company Internet sites may put you directly in touch with employees working for companies, through chat rooms and news-groups. Try to leave sensible questions which show interest, and check your e-mail regularly. You never know where such contacts could lead – even if the person you chat to isn't involved in management of the area you want to work in, he or she could send you in the direction of people who are. Employees can give you the nuts and bolts of what it's like to work in their job from one day to another. Personal profiles also give clues as to the sorts of opportunities such companies offer – and the sort of image they seek to portray. In some sites, you have a chance to chat online to find out what it's like to work there. Employees will tell you what it's really like, pros, cons and all.

Finding out about 'getting in'

ASK YOURSELF
How can I get to meet people in the heart of the sector and seek out their advice?

You can find out how to meet people working in the career you are thinking of moving into by seeking information from professional bodies, company Web sites or printed materials, attending careers events and talking to recruitment agencies.Questions to ask when you meet people include:

- What are the attitudes towards career changers? Do any employers actively seek to recruit them?
- What are employers looking for in staff and in new recruits?

- What does it take to get 'in'? What will you need to do to make yourself noticed?
- What will you need to do to give you the edge?
- What position might you expect to start in as somebody changing career who has experience of the workplace? (Some employers will expect you to begin at the level of an 18 or even 16-year-old, which could affect the salary you bring home.)
- Where might you expect to be in a year's time? Five years'?
- Are there any courses they suggest you take?
- Would they be willing to offer you a chance to do some work experience for a week, or spend a day or two shadowing people who do the job?
- What advice would they have for you overall?
- Is there anybody else they would suggest you talk to?
- Is there anything you're not doing that you should be doing to get a foot into the door?

NEXT STEP

Attend careers events.

Careers events provide useful opportunities to meet people face to face who work in the sector that interests you; they are an excellent way to make an impression and to network. They are attended by employers, professional bodies and educational establishments who want to recruit staff, and provide an excellent chance to compare what is on offer and consider how you might 'fit' into their cultures. Some fairs are generalist, such as the Evening Standard Job Scene and Graduate and Professional fair in London, and offer you the chance to talk to representatives from across the retail, finance, education, engineering and health-care sectors, as well as training providers. Others are sector specific, like the IT event VISIT. Careers fairs vary in size, from the small local event organized by some local organization such as a careers service, or local body of employers, to a major fair, such as the large higher education fairs which move around the country every year. Your local careers service will have details of events in your area, or you can visit www.careersfair.com for more information.

Careers fairs will enable you to gather information from different employers and compare what they have to offer. They also provide an opportunity to make contacts and to talk to people who might be interested in hiring you.

ASK YOURSELF
How can I make the most of this type of event?

Find out who will be attending the fair before you go from the event organizers, and target the stands that interest you most. When you arrive, visit them before you get too tired and hot, or your time at the event runs out. To make the most of the visit:

- Work out what you want to achieve out of it before you go.
- Plan some questions to ask to show that you're interested.
- Make use of any talks and sessions running alongside the event, which offer general advice on job hunting and writing a CV, or more specifically, what it's like to work in a particular sector.
- Dress appropriately as if you were going for an interview – first impressions count.
- Prepare up-to-date copies of your CV to show what you can do and what you want to do in the future.
- Prepare yourself to talk positively about why you're changing career, and describe the research you've done so far.

Other ways to make contact

Human contact tells us a great deal. Call up the company and ask for written leaflets outlining its products and services. Do they arrive promptly? How is your request handled? Do the staff sound interested and awake, or bored, or overworked? Does the company appear to produce the literature itself, or does it outsource that part of the operation?

Events such as careers or even trade fairs provide an excellent chance to meet people and follow up your meeting after you've met them. Visit any sales outfits or showrooms to see what you think of the staff. Some organizations also hold open days or evenings for interested potential recruits to look round and discuss career opportunities. They hold these events deliberately to throw the net wide open, to recruit the best staff they can. Go. Introduce yourself. Tell them what you're doing. Give them a copy of your CV and contact details. Follow up with a call or letter to thank them. Keep in touch.

It could also be worth talking to people who have strong contacts with the sector, such as recruitment agencies, to see what skills you will need to acquire. Again, many of these attend careers fairs with a view to meeting prospective people who will want to work for them.

Recruitment agencies

Recruitment agencies have an intensive network of contacts, within any given sector and locality. Some are specialist and focus on one specific career area, such as childcare, or financial services or hospitality positions, or secretarial. Others are more generalist, covering everything. Agencies play a key role in recruiting staff for many organizations, particularly small- and medium-sized employers who want to spend a minimum amount of time on the actual process of recruitment themselves. Recruitment agencies seek to put a select number of applicants forward for any position they have been asked to fill, bearing in mind the needs and requirements of the employers concerned. Good agencies know what employers out there want.

Agencies also bear in mind the needs of the individuals who come to them looking for work – people like you. They will take details of individuals seeking work and consider which vacancies on their files they would be suitable for. There should be no fee for the job seeker – the employer alone pays for any successful matching of employer and applicant.

Plus points about using agencies are:

- They should have a good overview of what the sector's recruitment needs are, and what sort of people employers are recruiting.
- Many agencies have Web sites. Visit a few until you find one you feel comfortable with, and Bookmark it.
- Agencies will be recruiting for live vacancies.
- They will have seen a wide variety of people come through the door and will be in a good position to tell you, as a person seeking to change career, what sort of things you will need to do to strengthen your chances of getting a job in your chosen field.
- They will be recruiting permanent positions, and will probably also have a temporary division, which, if you so choose and are able, can place you directly in the line of your chosen career.
- They will offer advice and interesting points about the workplace today.

Either on a person-to-person basis, or over the Internet, agencies and job sites such as www.workthing.com or www.reed.co.uk can give you information on topics along these lines:

- an indication of the salaries certain careers command;
- advice on job hunting, such as interview techniques, writing your CV;
- help with psychometric tests;
- online questionnaires to help you determine what you want in a job;
- a national or even international reach depending on their size and goals;
- advice on how to leave your present job;
- information on the Internet about issues relating to the workplace, such as trends, problems, growth areas, legal matters;
- ways in which you can improve your skills;
- what employers are looking for in a given area.

If you plan to use an agency to find work while changing career, ensure they are members of the Recruitment and Employment Confederation.

The media and the press

Scanning the pages of the press for jobs that might interest you is a traditional way of looking for work. Some are fairly general, in that they will have one main recruitment section a week, whereas others – like the _Guardian_ – have specific days devoted to particular sectors. (Monday, media; Tuesday, education; Wednesday, public and community jobs; Thursday, science and graduate). Today, most papers have Web sites and vacancy pages which will introduce you to national and international jobs, while others such as www.fish4jobs.co.uk compile vacancies from regional paper. A range of professional opportunities is available at www.ft.com. Some papers, such as _The Times_ have links with Web sites (in this case www.revolver.com).

Where papers really come into their own is in giving you an idea of what the trends and issues are within any given sector; you can read them over lunch in the office without anyone suspecting anything, or on the train. Items you see which particularly interest you give you something to talk about when you are meeting people who work in the sector you are hoping to go into. Additionally, the press offer advice and information on: job hunting; advice on courses; franchises; new government initiatives; trends in the workplace; recruitment methods; and details of job vacancies, internationally, nationally, in your region and locally, depending on the publication.

The BBC has a massive Web site at www.bbc.co.uk with information on careers, training and employment. In particular, it has a work skills site which covers all aspects of job hunting and career development, with a World of Work interest inventory which means you can match yourself against profiles of people in different jobs – and find out how they got in.

Personal contacts/network and friends/family

These can offer a powerful way to find out about careers and jobs, and, in particular, to hear of vacancies in areas that interest you. If you are going into a new career involving an interest, the chances are that you know people involved in that area already. Now is the time to make good use of your network and pull a few favours. You can always return those favours later.

Talk to people you meet who clearly enjoy their work, especially when you are out socially. Benefit from the fact that, even if it is a Saturday night and work for the week is forgotten, people love to talk about themselves and what they are doing. Find out what they enjoy about their jobs. 'How did you get into this, then?' If they changed career, ask what motivated them, and how they saw the whole thing through. You could pick up useful tips about financial support, although you should never assume that what applies to one person will automatically apply to you. Firstly, things change and secondly your own individual circumstances could be very different to the person you were talking to.

NEXT STEP

See if you can spend a day or more shadowing somebody who does the role or career you'd like to do.

'What can I learn in a day?' you may be asking. The answer is, more than you might think, if you prepare properly for the time you're going to spend with people. You have several opportunities here. First, you can get first-hand knowledge of what goes on, and see what the reality of working in a particular career (or at least, sector) is like. Second, you can make an impression and make contacts; tell those you're placed with what you've been doing to prepare for your career change. (What you're really telling them is that you're getting charged and skilled up to do the job.) Third, if you look back thoughtfully on what you've seen, you will have an opportunity to see how many transferable skills those people you saw working used; how they used them; and how you can show that you have them. Fourth, it will give you an idea as to what specific skills and knowledge you need to pick up in order to do the job you've seen.

This sort of exposure is particularly important if you're going for a career that will demand lengthy training before you can start work. If there are certain aspects of the job you cannot cope with, it's better to know at the start, rather than halfway through training. Make the most of the chance to:

- find out if it's for you or not;
- talk to people who actually do the work to find out what it's like;
- get a practical viewpoint;
- see what other people think of the industry;
- learn to speak their language and get to know their culture, which should increase your effectiveness at interviews;
- prove your interest to prospective employers;
- network;
- gauge how comfortable you felt in that sort of environment and sector.

If you're actually wishing to train for a specific career, your request to spend time with an organization will come as no surprise to it. Many employers are used to taking students on for short periods of time so that they can learn by doing (work experience) or learn by watching (work shadowing). Throughout the UK, students in schools, colleges and universities are participating in such programmes, which may last for a few weeks (one day a week) to up to a year in industry on a full-time basis. Consequently organizations are used to people joining them for all sorts of reasons for all periods of time – perhaps on a visit to see what the place is like, or to do a project towards course work. It's a useful PR exercise for the company involved, and it helps them promote the opportunities they have to offer – one day, one of these people could be working with them.

ASK YOURSELF

What bugs or downsides are there about this
career or role, and how do those affect me?

An important part of any research is to check out the advantages and
disadvantages of the work and to consider whether the cons annoy
you so much that it's best left to others to do. People doing the work
provide a useful insight into this area. This is an important time to
think about:

- the stressful sides to the work and how you would cope with
  these;
- whether you have any health problems like poor eyesight,
  colour-blindness or skin allergies which may block out
  some careers to you;
- whether there are any working conditions you're not
  prepared to put up with, such as horrible weather if you
  work outdoors, heights, blood, and vomit;
- what the issues are facing those who work in the sector, and
  how you would handle them.

Information on training and courses

NEXT STEP

**Find out courses or training you'll need to take to
get to where you want to be, or that will boost
your chances of securing a job in your new career.**

Professional bodies can provide lots of information about the
training required to enter a career, and the professional qualifications available once you are in it. Many are actively involved in the

work of Sector Skills Councils, whose role it is to ensure that the business and skills needs of a sector are met, so that it does not suffer from a lack of trained and qualified workers.

If you're going to train for a new career, find out what resources you'll need in terms of time, money and brain power to train for it;

- Contact professional bodies for details of what is required and also see if they can point you in the direction of training providers.
- Obtain information from training providers on the courses they run.
- Talk to students on the courses to find out exactly what the courses entail in terms of their content, methods of assessment and the likely time commitment required per week, so you have an idea of what you will need to put in over and above your current working day (and whether you are prepared to fulfil that commitment).
- Work out what it would cost.
- Find out whether your present experience and knowledge would short-cut any of the courses available (see Chapter 8).

Top Tip

Education and training courses provide the facility
to train for a new career... often without leaving home!

ASK YOURSELF

How do I see myself studying and retraining?
What time can I afford to give?

Could you consider:

Yes/No

Part time courses, held during the day or in the
evening, for one or two days or nights a week: ———

Intensive courses give you the skills you
need fast, within a shortened period of time,
for example over six months instead of a year: ———

Short courses – a morning, or a Saturday
(for example many colleges hold Saturday
courses) or over the course of a week
in a sort of summer-school arrangement: ———

Taster courses to give you an idea of what
a career involves and to start building the skills
and abilities you will need to gain an
edge in the employment market: ———

Modular courses enable you to take one course
one term, then have a term off studying if that
is what suits you: ———

Full time courses mean just that: you are expected
to study five days a week as if you were working,
so you would probably study on your own
and attend lectures for 40 hours a week: ———

Distance learning courses are designed to fit in
with you: you cover a set core of subjects
within a course, designed by a tutor or academic
institution, but you can study at home by
correspondence or by learning online: ———

Open learning means you decide what you want
to learn, how you wish to learn it and when. ———

Tremendous strides have been made to encourage individuals to develop a lifelong approach to learning, chiefly by increasing access to every individual. In Britain, the University of Industry has provided training at a time and a place to suit the learner, perhaps at home, or at work or through a national network of training centres. The development of NVQs (SVQs in Scotland) has provided for a range of practical qualifications which allow you to learn skills for the workplace. NVQs differ from academic qualifications in that:

- you don't have to sit exams – you are assessed at work, in a voluntary placement, or in a work-simulated environment;
- they can be completed at a speed to suit you;
- they focus on your ability to apply practical skills, ie they are all hands-on stuff and testify that you are competent to do certain tasks at work;

'There are courses for the person who wants to change career – full time, part time, distance learning, online learning. It's a matter of finding the right one. And there are Web sites to help you do that quickly.'

The following are examples of some of these Web sites:

www.ucas.ac.uk – for degree and Higher National Diploma courses; it may be necessary to attend a full academic degree course in order to change your career to occupations such as veterinary science, engineering, dentistry and physiotherapy. You may consider the best route for you is to study a course full time for two, three or four years immersed in the area you want to take up professionally. There are plenty of vocational courses on offer, from graphic design to forestry, and fisheries management to social work. Ensure the course has sufficient links with employers and use the holidays to gain relevant work experience to enhance your chances of landing work after you graduate.

www.prospects.ac.uk or **www.hobsons.com** – for postgraduate courses; many courses provide an opportunity for graduates to change career and go into areas such as law, teaching, hotel management, careers advisory work, recreational management and human resources. Others will provide you with the opportunity to specialize in your chosen area to a considerable degree.

If you have considered a postgraduate course, remember there are many full-time, part-time and distance-learning courses which can provide a stepping stone into other careers. Try to find a course that has strong links with employers and involves work experience to enhance your employment prospects. Both Web sites mentioned above can help in finding the right course and both give information about that important subject: *funding it*. Don't ignore the fantastic range of short courses available throughout the UK which can provide you with the knowledge and qualifications you need to change career.

www.hotcourses.com – for short courses and those at the further education level.

www.learndirect.co.uk – provides many courses online, so it doesn't matter where you live, you will be able to find a course. You can call Learn Direct too (see Useful addresses and further information).

www.floodlight.co.uk – this is really for people seeking to study in the London area, although it gives a useful insight into the sorts of classes now available. You can study a very wide range of subjects at all different levels and this site is worth a look just so you can get an idea of what is possible in a short time.

www.odlqc.org.uk – an accrediting body which assures quality control for distance-learning courses covering a wide range of subjects delivered by such colleges as the National Extension College, the London School of Journalism and Mercers College.

Colleges and universities all have Web sites, detailing their full- and part-time courses. They all have careers services to help you find the right course and job for you, and in fact many have adult guidance centres dedicated to helping adults specifically. Many colleges and universities offer short courses on a huge range of subjects, including soft skills such as presentation skills and interview techniques.

Many libraries and careers services offer access to databases of training courses with information on what is available in your local area on a full-time, part-time and short-course basis.

Further advice and guidance

'I really would like to sit down with somebody and just talk through my ideas. Where can I find a careers adviser?'

The growth of careers choice has been matched by the development of courses and access to information, advice centres and careers advisory companies. In the UK, careers services have now been privatized. Now called Connexions, they provide advice, help and information to young people aged 13–19 on a whole range of issues. The helpline Learn Direct has advisers to help adults; you can also visit its Web Site at www.learndirect.co.uk, where there are many job profiles and also an opportunity to analyse your skills and interests to find a new career.

The British Psychology Society can send you a list of qualified members offering vocational guidance to adults for which you will probably pay for a session. Alternatively, you can look in your phone book. One of the better known companies, whose advertisements are frequently seen in the press, is called Career Analysts, based in London. Many people use life coaches to help them achieve their goals. You can turn to the Internet, too, for many Web sites give you the chance to match yourself against careers. Such an opportunity is offered by www.prospects.ac.uk.

If you have an interview with a careers adviser, don't expect to come out with your life sorted. A careers adviser's job is to help you explore your thinking, and to broaden your horizons, and help you determine what is right for you – but not to tell you what to do. Careers advisers act as a sounding board against which you can pitch your ideas; they can challenge your thoughts. You must think about what you want, and who you are, and put the ground work in.

103

It takes time to work out what you want to do – it's not something you can do overnight.

'What are my other options if I want to change career - I mean things like working for yourself, buying a franchise and doing voluntary work for time out? Where can I get details on those?'

Many colleges have courses for people seeking to run their own business, when there is usually a representative from a bank or building society to give financial advice. You may be able to share equipment and facilities with others going down a similar route, through tele-centres. Alternatively, your own business could be based on somebody else's premises, such as a catering outlet set up in a local college to provide food to staff and students. Again, there are niches here: would one specialize in sandwiches, or be a hot potato outlet – or offer both?

ASK YOURSELF

What would I need to consider if
I wanted to run my own business?

Questions you might ask yourself include:

- Is anybody else offering this service or product?
- Is the area already overloaded with the type of business you are thinking of running?
- How could you provide something that is different from the other companies, yet still speaks of quality and a personal service?
- How would you cope with the routine tasks other people might previously have done for you?
- How will your family manage if you work from home?

- How would this fit in from a purely practical point of view? Where would you work and store your papers?
- Matters such as national and local business rates, building regulations, rental costs, insurance, data protection and confidentiality – how can you protect confidentiality of your clients from your flatmates/partner/children?
- The facilities you would need – e-mail, fax, the Internet, laptop, filing cabinet, etc.
- How would you operate – as a sole trader, partnership or public limited company?
- What would your business plan and marketing strategy be (you will need both if you want to convince a bank or building society to lend you money to start you off).
- What are your charges going to be for your products and/or services.
- How would you build up a track record and track trends and new developments?

ASK YOURSELF

How quickly could I start doing this, even part-time, as a new career?

Finally, consider how quickly you would make money. Could you start working while you are still in your current job, using weekends and evenings to get started? Self-employment might not be an immediate option – it could be a goal for the future:

1. Get experience and a network of customers while working for somebody else.
2. Make a name for yourself.
3. Find a gap in the market – your 'niche'.
4. Do the research to formulate a business plan.
5. Arrange the financing.
6. You are in business!

For more details on working from home, visit www.work-ingfromhome.co.uk, a site from British Telecom. It has a lot of information on the benefits and problems of working from home, with practical help on day-to-day issues. Additionally, you can contact your local Business Link (England), Business Connect (Wales) and Business Shop (Scotland); these three entities can help those seeking to start their own business by giving them much useful information, particularly relevant to the locality.

'I'd like to run my own business – but I'd be happier with some support behind me.'

Think about buying a franchise operation. People who buy franchises do so with the knowledge that they have been tried and tested elsewhere and that they will receive training and support, together with the right to operate exclusively in a given area – you will not be working in direct competition with another franchisee. You can buy a franchise from £5,000 to £100,000, so they cover many budgets. Most offer good training and support. There are franchises in all sorts of sectors, such as pet food distribution, running recruitment companies, managing sandwich chains, and cleaning operations.

For more information on franchising: contact the British Franchise Association (see Useful addresses and further information); attend the British Franchise Association fairs, held in cities such as London, Manchester, Glasgow and Birmingham throughout the year; or look out for National Franchise Week, usually well promoted in the business and career pages of the press.

The most important elements to consider when researching franchise operations are:

- How much will it cost?
- What sort of support and backup is there?
- How much management experience do you need?
- How much will it affect your home life?
- Why are the franchise operators seeking to set up in your area at that time?
- How soon can you expect to recoup your investment?
- Is the franchiser a member of the British Franchise Association?

- How long has the franchise been running for? Who else can you talk to who is involved other than the central coordinator?
- Insist on seeing the franchise accounts, whatever state you are told the finances are in.

Banks and building societies may have staff dedicated to advising those setting up their own business or seeking to run a franchise. Your public library's reference section will contain industry and sector reports. Many libraries have staff dedicated to help businesses do research, so enlist their help.

'I want to do something for the good of others.'

You may have an idea that you want to put into practice such as organizing an event, or setting up a group to help others. Look around carefully for possible sponsors. For inspiration, read Charles Handy's *The New Alchemists... How Visionary People make Something out of Nothing.* Consider TimeBank, whereby you share your time and skills for the benefit of the community by depositing some time with the TimeBank. You tell them what you are interested in doing and have a passion for – for example, human and civil rights, mental health, politics, animals – and what skills and experience you would like to use – driving, fund-raising, teaching – and how far you can travel and when you would like to start, and they find and send you a list of opportunities that appeal to your passions plus details of organizations in your locality which can help. You could set up an initiative of your own. For more details on TimeBank, see Useful addresses and further information.

Summary exercises

Based on the research you have done in the last two chapters, note down:

1. Which sorts of sectors are involved in the sort of work that interests me and where I can make a difference in the way I want?

2. Which careers will enable me to use the skills and knowledge I want to use?
3. What would I have to do to get into that sector?
4. Where are there gaps in my area where I might start my own business and use my skills?
5. What opportunities are really starting to appear as possible new careers? (Remember, this will take time to work out.)

6 'Should I? Shouldn't I? It's decision time'

It's decision time!

> ### At this stage, you may be thinking:
>
> Yes, I am going to change career and this is
> what I am going to do next.   _____
>
> Yes, I think I will change career – I have got
> four or five options and I need to just think
> about those more.   _____
>
> I want to shift career as opposed to changing it.
> Is there anything I can do where I am now
> to achieve that move?   _____
>
> My current job seems to offer much of what
> I want. I need to develop a new way of
> approaching it.   _____

To help you decide whether or not to go ahead and change career,
this chapter is intended to encourage you to focus on these questions:

1. How closely do the opportunities you have been looking at
   fit with what you want?
2. How can you afford to change career?
3. How will you benefit if you do?
4. What will happen if you don't change career?
5. What does your gut instinct tell you?

Consider each question carefully and work out the answers *as they relate to you and to your own situation*. Look at your answers overall. What are they telling you? What is your gut instinct telling you?

ASK YOURSELF

How closely do prospective opportunities fit with what I want in my chosen career?

Look closely at how each option meets the elements that together create a job: the motivation to do it, the skills, knowledge, qualities and training required, your lifestyle aspirations and your preferred method of working. Use any scale you like to measure this match: number from one (excellent match) to five (nowhere near), if you want; or use words to describe the match (spot on... miles apart).

- What would you have to do to get from where you are now to attain that option?
- How much would any training cost? Would it be essential to take time out to achieve the change? Is that a feasible option?
- What opportunities are there locally?
- How soon could you start working towards each option? The contract you have with your current employer may mean you cannot work for anybody else, but that does not mean you cannot start contacts in your proposed career area, making contacts, attending events, reading around the industry.
- How far would each provide you with the sort of lifestyle you (and your dependants) want?
- Where there are gaps between your ideals and the opportunity, do they matter to you that much? Can you overcome them in any way? Or are you best to discard that opportunity?
- What sort of salary can you expect to earn? (Don't weep over this point if it is considerably lower than your current income. This chapter will turn to financial planning in a minute.)

ASK YOURSELF
How do these options compare with my current job?

Now do the same for your current job to see how much of a match there is. If there is a substantial gap between what you have discovered about yourself and your current job, it will be very difficult to remain in your current job. If your present job is not a million miles away from what you want at work, perhaps you need to do some tweaking to it and make more effort where you are. Are you really taking the initiative and control to ensure that your job is as fulfilling, exciting and rewarding as it should be? Challenge yourself to be more pro-active in making a go of the job you're in now.

If you like what you have found out about your career prospects, and it really means something to you and hits home, listen to your heart. It will be even harder to keep doing the job you are in from now on, if what you have seen is right for you.

ASK YOURSELF
How can I afford to change career if it involves a massive drop in salary?

Lots of people have changed career and survived well and far more happily on considerably lower salaries than they were previously bringing home. Look at the following list (see box p.112), which contains things most people see as essentials, and add any others you think necessary. Jot down how much you spend on them now. Then _really make an effort_ to find out how much you can cut them down to an absolute minimum. Practise cutting down for a couple of months. Put anything you save into a savings account or use the money to pay off any debts (like credit cards).

	£/week or month	
	Now	*Absolute minimum*
Essentials		
food	_____	_____
warmth	_____	_____
electricity/gas	_____	_____
water bill	_____	_____
rates	_____	_____
tax	_____	_____
telephone bill	_____	_____
car costs	_____	_____
clothes	_____	_____
rent/mortgage	_____	_____
insurance	_____	_____
essential toiletries	_____	_____
getting to work	_____	_____
medicines	_____	_____
first other _____	_____	_____
second other _____	_____	_____

Look at the sort of salary you could earn in your proposed new career, both while gaining experience and once you are up to 'full speed' in the job, and ask yourself:

- Based on the amount we have just cut down, could I/we live on this income?
- Where could I/we economize further?
- How could I/we make my/our money go further?
- How would I/we benefit financially?

The last point is important. If you change career, you could find yourself paying less money on:

- tax and national insurance if you are in a lower tax bracket (find out from your local tax office what that would be);

- commuting costs, if any;
- the sort of wardrobe you need to wear for the job you are in now;
- socializing with workmates or colleagues and clients.

ASK YOURSELF

How will I personally benefit
overall from a career change?

The next list really gives you the chance to create a vision of your future life and how it might be if you changed career for yourself. Career change can be blocked by an individual failing to visualize how different their life might be as a whole if they changed career. Before you complete the next box's right-hand column, try to justify your 'nice to have list', or 'important to me' as they are to you right now. What effect do they have on you? Perhaps they help you de-stress. If you changed your career and had a job you enjoyed and that didn't stress you out so much, could you manage without them? Could the weekend and evening walks in the countryside (free) replace the gym membership (costs)? Would you still need them if you changed career and were doing something you found more enjoyable and fulfilling?

Important to me	Essential	Nice to have	I would replace it with/How I would cope without it
private health insurance	_____	_____	_____
pension plan	_____	_____	_____
holiday	_____	_____	_____
golf membership	_____	_____	_____

tennis club	_____	____	_____
classic car	_____	____	_____
school fees	_____	____	_____
designer clothes	_____	____	_____
eating out	_____	____	_____
gym membership	_____	____	_____
entertainment			_____
alcohol (at home/out)	_____	____	_____
cigarettes	_____	____	_____
magazine subscriptions	_____	____	_____
charity donations	_____	____	_____
club memberships	_____	____	_____
first other	_____	____	_____
second other	_____	____	_____

Looking at the above list, identify what you would get rid of if your proposed career change meant a dramatic change in your financial situation. If it meant you were happy at work, instead of being a whingeing miserable soul, wouldn't it be worth it? Think not just about what you are losing (massive salary, eating out, fabulous lifestyle etc) but what you are gaining (job you enjoy and value, more time with friends/family, to enjoy hobbies). Ask yourself how much of your current job is a reflection of the people you work with and their expectations of what you do in your free time. Dare to live your life differently.

To take an example, let us say your career change would involve working 30 minutes from home because that is where the opportunities would be, as opposed to the two-hour journey you have at present. Your thoughts may run something like this:

At the moment, I have a two hour journey to get to work.
I do not like the job, but the money is very good.
I spend about £2,700 a year on the journey.
I get to work feeling as if I've done a full day's work already.
If I change career, I'll get a job locally.
It would take, say, 30 minutes to get to work.
I'd love the job – but the money wouldn't be brilliant.
However, I'd save money on commuting.
I'd get to work ready to do a good day's work.
I'd be less stressed, irritated and happier.
I'd gain three hours of my life back for things I want to do. How would I fill those three hours?

To help you make the right decision, weigh up:

If I change career

The things I would gain

The things I would lose

greater self-esteem
– I have changed career!

I have boosted my employability
skills

greater job satisfaction because
of what I am doing at work

more time with the children

lower salary

less stress – better health without
the level of responsibility

would I miss the level of
responsibility?

no commuting – more time for
me to do what I want, not
spending money on the commute

would I miss being able
to go to smart restaurants
with clients in the City?

I'll get my evenings
– my life – back.

more energy – better sex life!	will have to drop membership of gym
go walking at weekends, take up cycling	
more interesting job I love – 48 weeks of the year	lose a job I hate – can I really see myself doing this for much longer and for 48 weeks of each year?
less stress as I'm doing a job I enjoy – so would I need so many treats?	have to cut back on luxury holidays, eating out, all those treats I needed before when I was so stressed and had so little time for me
tremendously enriched life	

Take time to complete the exercise on page 114–116. It contains the details that help you paint a picture of how different your life could be, so do not just say 'I gain three hours'. Tell yourself how you would use that time, and what you would do with it. Create a picture of how different your life would be if you changed career.

ASK YOURSELF

What will happen if I do not change?

Do not just ask yourself what the implications are if you do change career. Think of what could happen if you *do not*. Turn the 'what ifs' into positive energy – or threats. The implications of not switching career are probably as frightening as doing it. So which of the following do you think would apply to you if you stayed in the same job for the next five years, ie you stay put?

	Yes/No

My performance at work will get worse. _____

I'll regret it. _____

I will always wonder what would have happened if I had gone through with changing career. _____

I'll end up doing things I do not want to do for years. _____

I'll be with people perhaps I do not want to be with, or even like. _____

Other people will probably end up making a decision for me. _____

The company might pick up on my lack of enthusiasm and fire me. _____

The sooner I learn to cope with change, the better. _____

If I can make this change, there will be other things I can do, too. _____

I will be happier in myself if I could change career. _____

I will be disappointed with myself if I do not. _____

I want to drive change, rather than be blown along by it. _____

I will be safe but bored for the next five years. _____

Would I regret it if I didn't try? _____

I will waste a lot of my working life doing something I do not enjoy. _____

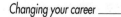

Top Tip

Do not be another *'if only'* statistic.
Life is for living.

ASK YOURSELF

What does my gut instinct tell me?

Only you know the answer to this one. Listen to your gut instinct –
what is it telling you? Now look at your answers to the questions
thus far in this chapter. Weigh them up. Do they back up your gut
instinct? Is your gut instinct and heart telling you to change all the
time? Does that feeling ever go away or is it there, over your
shoulder, as you work?

Still not convinced?

'My gut instinct says, I should go for this career change. Why am I still dithering?'

The motivation to make the change happen is an essential ingre-
dient in making a successful career change. You can wait, ponder,
think and research all you like. But sooner or later, you have to
decide whether to make the change or not. There is almost a fear of
'what if this really works and I've hit the jackpot and I love it and I'm
brilliant at it?' There is also the fear of change – how much will your
life be affected by changing career? There's a certain thrill to
changing career, not least the excitement – will you sink or swim?
Will it work? Will you hate it? What if you really, really love it? Will
you regret you didn't make the change earlier? (Most people do.)

If you can picture yourself in your new career, and have a strong vision of succeeding in it, and living a far happier life, you are far more likely to make the move – and do it successfully. The more you believe that it will happen, the more likely it is that it will. Picture yourself in it first thing in the morning, last thing at night. Spend time alone during the week, thinking of yourself in your new career. Have faith in yourself and your ability to make the change.

'How should I tell people who – I know – are going to be shocked that I want to change career?'

Tell them you are changing career, explain very clearly why and do not let them dissuade you. You have decided it is time to do something that is important to you, and you will be far more effective at work as a result. Maturity gives us the confidence to cope with family nagging, handle expectations others have of you, and ensure you will be all right financially. Talk to friends you trust first about your proposed change, so that you can get used to the idea yourself, gain some practice telling people and receive positive and enthusiastic comments on your proposed plans, so that, when the less than helpful people start up, you will know they are just wallowing in negativity in their usual way.

'I have dependants, and their circumstances are going to make this change difficult to achieve. Is there any way around this?'

If you have elderly relatives or youngsters at home who need your help, check that you are fully up to date with all the public and private support available in your area to you, both within the home and outside it, such as day care centres, sitting services and residential homes. Retain your focus and see how far you switch career anyway. Be creative in your problem solving and talk to others in the same boat to see how they are coping. When people see you are really serious about switching career, and they see it means something to you, often they become tremendous supporters because they do not want to be the reason you couldn't do it.

'I guess my own situation could put restrictions on me'

Your future career plans could be restricted by dependants who rely on you, such as elderly relatives, or children, or your current location. Talk to your partner (and children) about their own plans which could, for example, make relocating impossible. If there is not a lot of scope in your area for the sector in which you are considering working in, consider how mobile you (and your dependants) are, and whether you are willing to move to another area to boost your chances of finding a new job. This is a major decision, not to be taken lightly, and you should discuss this with those living with you who rely on you.

'What will people say?'

Don't let pride get in the way of happiness at work. You have every right to a job you enjoy and take pride in. If people are critical, it is possibly because you will have achieved something they would never have dared to do themselves. Do not worry what others think. At the end of the day, focus on what you will gain by changing career and ask yourself if they really have any idea of what is involved, either in the process of change or in the job you are planning to do itself.

Cut down on the time you spend with people who aren't positive about your proposed career change. You need to be around people who are going to boost your self-esteem and self-belief, not belittle you. You know what makes you happy. Show them you deserve better than the life of mediocrity they apparently would like you to lead if you stay in the job you're in now.

Finally, ask yourself again how used you are to change. If you're a bit of a stick in the mud, used to your daily and weekly routines, practise moving away from what's safe in your life.

'I think the whole thing is too risky. So what else can I do?'

You may still decide you cannot afford to take the risk to move to a new career. Use all the information you have gathered about yourself and the workplace. If you think you really need to stay with your current company, make a list of the benefits of doing so. Build on the positive elements and make a plan for the next six months to enhance your employability in the market and make your job more interesting and satisfying. See if it is possible to redirect your job in the direction of the career you really want, by taking on projects that are going to expand your knowledge and skills base, and networking widely in your sector and perhaps getting involved in local groups that discuss local issues.

You can also try to make life outside of work more enjoyable by starting new hobbies or interests, doing some voluntary work in a career area that interests you, and paying off your debts and saving money. The more you put into your life outside of work, the less you will focus on the job itself.

ASK YOURSELF

How else can I put life into my career?

Some of the suggestions below may appeal more to your company than others and some may be easier to fulfil if you're working for a larger company as opposed to a small one:

- shifting career, eg moving from nursing to teaching nursing;
- changing to another culture, eg moving from the public sector to the private;
- specializing, eg going from nursing to midwifery;
- moving jobs, eg moving from one hospital to another;
- going on secondment;
- having a career break;
- taking a sabbatical;
- taking your skills and expertise abroad, for organizations such as the VSO;
- taking on a job that demands less of your time so you can put spark into your spare time by doing things that interest you.

'How does a career shift differ from a career change?'

Let us start with an example. Judy, a personal and social education teacher, shifted career by leaving the classroom to work for the local education authority, organizing all work experience placements for all the schools in the area. This meant she moved from spending time teaching to working closely with local companies and schools in the county, where her teaching experience came in useful but she was able to also develop her expertise and focus on her interest in strengthening the relationship between industry and education.

Career shifts may also be useful stepping stones to long-term goals. For example, David, a specialist in marine biology, wanted to write coffee-table books, but he wanted to have complete control over the content. To take photographs that would be acceptable to a publisher, he ran a photography shop for two years. He learnt about the whole business of photography but also the retail industry: what sold, what didn't. Eventually, his abilities had progressed to such a level that he was indeed able to publish a marine biology book with his own words and photographs. He had shifted career to get to where he wanted to be, but kept sight of his original goals.

If you are contemplating a career switch, you should keep this opportunity to shift career in mind. Don't spend all your time 'pubbing and clubbing'. Do something meaningful. The more you get involved, the richer your life will be.

'I could do a gradual move to a new career, couldn't I?'

Depending on what sort of career you are moving to, you could start spending less time in the job you are on now, allowing you time to train for your new career and even to pick up work experience on the days you are not working. (This would not apply if the career is one that demands a four-year degree course which is rigorously spelt out by the professional body overseeing its training and educational requirements.) Can you imagine:

- moving from five days a week on the job to four?
- working from home on one day a week?
- temping or doing contract work?
- working freelance, eg while at work, depending on the nature of your move?

- taking two part-time jobs and becoming a portfolio worker – working in your old field for a while and taking a part-time job in your new career?

Gradual career moves

Mandy went part-time with her current employer on the basis that she would train up a replacement, whom she identified with her line manager.

Peter left and went freelance for a while to keep the money coming in, during the time he was training for his new career.

Roger did consultancy work for one year to get sufficient money to train for his new role.

Sarah moved to a four-day week to give herself one day to devote entirely to her new career. She woke at the normal time and worked a usual working day – nine to six.

Get on with it! If you get stuck, it can be very difficult to move on – so keep moving your thinking forward.

Top Tip

Don't get stuck and bogged down in your decision making.

NEXT STEP
Just get on with it!

Nina was temping in London as a secretary, then applied for a 12 week course to train as a journalist. 'I could have gone on temping and trying to pay off my credit card forever,' she said, 'but sooner or later you have to make the break and have a cut-off point. I'd had a couple of articles published, which I sent in with my application for the course, so that helped show I was committed and knew what I was letting myself in for. And I applied for and got a career development loan to help me fund the course.'

To change career successfully, you must be:

1. prepared to study and train;
2. highly motivated;
3. absolutely committed to the change;
4. determined to see it through.

You must also have belief that you can, and will, make the change.

Summary exercises

1. What would be the best thing that would happen if you changed career?
2. Which would you rather be doing in six months' time: your present job or your new career?
3. Could you live with yourself if you went to your grave knowing you didn't try and you didn't give it a go?
4. Weigh up the money considerations against the thought of being a slave to the treadmill. Do you really want to let things be, or give yourself a challenge; move out of that easy ride and go where the going is unknown?

Top Tip

Don't fill your life with regrets;
fill it with 'at least I gave it a go'.
You will probably find you can add '*and* I was successful'.

---

7 Make the change your personal goal. Get on with it!

Focus on what is important

```
───────────────── Top Tip ─────────────────

    We all need to have our own particular goals to work
                        for in life.
    Make your career change your personal project.
```

If you have set yourself the goal to change your career, or at the very least drive your career to work in a particular sector, you will probably find you have gained a tremendous sense of relief and anticipation. In life, the process of working towards goals really helps us to feel fulfilled and purposeful. Without goals, you lack a sense of direction and purpose and the world passes you by without your taking any notice of what is going on in it, so it is not surprising that many of us look back over the year on New Year's Eve thinking, 'Where did the year go?' and wonder what we have to show for it. When planning your career, you need to alter your attitude to careership and put it on a higher plane than other things in your life. Putting the way forward down on paper can be a really good way to see the way forward. In other words, create an action plan.

Action plan

NEXT STEP

Create your own action plan to help you through your career change.

An action plan will help you realize what you are working towards and how long you are likely to take to complete the necessary preparation. It will give you an idea of what sort of timescale you are working towards and give you time to prepare financially. It will stop you getting disheartened and act as a memory jogger. If at times your career change seems a long way off in reality, you will know that you have started to make the change by doing something about it. Chapters 7 to 10 will help you prepare and carry out your action plan.

Based on the research you have done, and where you are headed, draw up an action plan along the following lines. Do not expect to be able to fill out the latter half of the plan straight away – use Chapters 8 and 9 to complete those.

Action plan

Where am I now?	Make a note of your qualifications, achievements, experience, transferable skills, job-specific skills knowledge and contacts thus far. Highlight those that are particularly relevant to your new career.
Where do I want to be?	Note down what you want to achieve.

What do I need to do to get there?	From the research you have done thus far, note down what you need to acquire in the way of:
	
	  – training;
	  – qualifications;
	  – contacts;
	  – the right skills base;
	  – experience/shadowing;
	  – voluntary work.

How can I do it?	How much time can you devote to your career change by acquiring knowledge, skills and contacts? Could you leave your current job, if you have one, and devote yourself full-time to your career change? (Would you have to do that? Many career changes can be achieved while you are still working.) Or will you have to keep working full-time and work towards your career change on a part-time basis?
What support will I need?	Simplify your life so that your career change receives your focused attention. Tell family and friends how they can help. Boost finances and clear debts. How much can you save to prepare for any downsizing of your income (if there is to be one)? Keep healthy.

How can I look for work?	When and how does this sector recruit? When should you start looking? How should you secure work?
How long will this take?	When can you expect to start working in your new career?
How am I going to... celebrate?	Hmm...

To change career successfully, you need to focus on your goals over a period of time rather like an Olympic athlete. They train for say four years, sometimes for as little as 10 seconds of glory. They have highly developed, focused goals and dedicate their lives to achieving them. They do not waste any energy, time or money on trivia. They have a 100 per cent self-belief that they will achieve their goal. If you are to achieve a career change, similarly to an athlete you will need to put in sustained activity, work and dedication over a period of time. If you are half-hearted about it and spend too many evenings watching television or downing pints at the local pub, you may have a good social life, but your career change will be pushed back further into the future.

Chapter 8 will show you how you can prepare for a new career, but in the meantime things you should allow time for in your action plan are:

- taking the appropriate training courses and acquiring any relevant qualifications;
- finding a company that will let you shadow somebody doing the job you would like to do – even if it is only for one day: this is especially the case if you want to train for a specific career;
- doing voluntary work with the people you would like to be working with to show that you can relate to them and their needs, especially if you have chosen to work with a specific group of people and need to prove that you have the ability

to empathize with them and work with them and build up an awareness of the sorts of problems they face;
- boosting your network and continuing to learn as much as you can about the sector.

The more you do to start spending your time on your new career, the better because you will start thinking you are in that new role already. Move to shape your current job and shift it towards your new role where you can.

'So when am I supposed to do all this preparation to change career? Life is hectic enough as it is...'

A dream ideal is to have time out to prepare for a career change. For most of us, this luxury isn't an option. The advantage of continuing to work is that you can keep in touch with the workplace (which moves fairly rapidly), and in particular, technology (which moves even faster) and even try to move your job in a direction such that you can develop skills you will need for your new career. The course you want to study may involve a full-time degree course at university, in which case you may need to look for a career closely related to what you wanted to do, or take out a personal loan to see yourself through the harder times. What can you do to buy yourself more time in a busy schedule?

ASK YOURSELF

Can I change the way I work to give
me more time to change my career?

One possibility is to reduce the number of hours you are working with your current employer, so that you can find time to prepare for your new career. If you are going to do this, stress the ways in which the company can benefit when you present your case and be very sure of how it would work. Do not pretend there are no disadvantages, because there will be some. If you are going to ask for any degree of flexible working, in order to succeed you must portray any such reality as being beneficial *to the company*. Always make yourself available at the end of your mobile phone. The flexible approach works both ways. Show you can keep your end of the arrangement and you are more likely to gain extra freedom of movement. If you get what you want, always, always show willing by being available on the end of your mobile phone. Check your voice-mail and e-mails regularly and respond rapidly.

'I need to keep working – but I'm determined to find the time to change career. Any thoughts?'

Many of us need to keep working, even on a part-time basis, while we plot our career change and then time is in very short supply. Yes, I know, it is easy to say, but if something is really important to you, you will find the time you need to do it. Many would-be authors, for example, write into the early hours of the morning, purely for the love of what they are doing. Once you have started to put time aside and got into the habit of using it for the purpose of study or, more broadly, working on a career change, you will soon get used to sticking to that time. It doesn't take long to change the habit, provided you stick to it at first when the going is tough. Instead of feeling exhausted after a working day, you feel excited and itch to get to work on your own, personal project which, if successful, will change the quality of your life in ways you would never have thought possible.

Finding extra time can be hard at first, so here are some suggestions:

- Map the way you spend your time for one week.
- Circle wasted time, for example: watching that programme just because you couldn't be bothered to do anything else; doing nothing on a train journey into work; waiting to provide a taxi service for the children; being hung-over.
- Look at ways in which you might 'buy time' by delegating, eg ordering groceries on the Internet.
- Delegate chores at home to your children.
- Create time by leaving work on time two days a week so that you gain an extra hour at home.

Ten minutes found will buy you the time you need to:

- contact professional bodies for details of new courses;
- call your local college to arrange a time to meet with a tutor to discuss a course;
- review ways you can cut costs – what is least important to you in your life?
- study the adverts in a local paper.

Twenty minutes will buy you time to:

- cover the part of the paper most relevant to the sector to pick up names of employing organizations, issues and trends, and matters concerning customers and clients;
- look at advertised jobs, researching the recruiter needs and seeing how you match up at first glance;
- think of examples in your life history to show you have the skills an employer looking to recruit you will want.

Get rid of the chaos and trivia in your life. Devote a weekend to reorganize yourself, tidying up, stocking up and discarding as much of everything you have no need for anymore, and doing all those odd jobs you have been promising to do for ages; those letters you have been meaning to write. At the end of the weekend, you will find your mind feels a lot clearer, because you will have less clutter to muddle through; and you can pay attention to what really matters.

Top Tip

Find an average of two hours a day
to focus on your career change
and you will acquire two working days every week
to change your career.

However, if you do not waste a single minute at present because you live life to the full, something is going to have to be pushed out – even if it is only until your career change has been achieved – to make way for your career change. You can always go back to whatever it is later. Rank the activities you would normally do during the week in order of importance but include changing your career. Stop doing the ones which are least important to you – delegate them if you have to do them.

Do not let anything interrupt you when you are working on your career change:

1. Obtain and use an answerphone.
2. Tell the children to answer the phone; train them to take messages.
3. Tell your friends what you are doing and ask them not to call at 'your' time; if they do, arrange a time for you to call back for a chat.
4. Stick to your guns. People will soon realize you are serious. Once you have stopped interruptions disturbing you a few times, it becomes far easier to keep doing it.
5. Be prepared to say no. Don't waste time giving people reasons or excuses.

Build up your support systems

Changing your career can provide a useful time to do a form of MOT, to check on the state of your life. How do you manage and cope with stress? What are your finances like? Have you got a back-up team to support you?

Manage your stress levels

Changing your career can be stressful and very tiring, as perhaps you continue to work and maintain normality while secretly plotting a new career and hoping the boss does not begin to suspect. It is important not to run out of steam and patience halfway through, so:

- Talk to people who will listen to you and be constructive, but not be too sympathetic. Nobody said changing career was going to be easy.
- Keep fit. Exercise relieves stress and boosts your mental capacity for alertness and thought. Walking is particularly

useful. Take the stairs instead of the lift. Try to incorporate exercise into your working day.

- Get plenty of sleep.
- Don't overdo the alcohol. I am not saying, do not drink. Just reduce the amount you consume. Caroline and Mike cut back on their red wine consumption; they both saved money, lost pounds and gained energy and an alertness which showed.
- Set yourself stretching goals, but ones you will achieve.
- Expect yourself to change as a person. You are on a journey of self-discovery and you are bound to be affected by what you are learning and finding out. Expect, too, your relationship with loved ones to change as you alter as a person.
- Make sure you find time to do fun things with those who are most important to you, so that they can keep up with the changing you, and you do not grow too much apart.
- If problems appear early on, find solutions by tackling them early. Talk to someone who can help.

Boost your support network

Friends and supporters are crucial at times like this to support and constantly give you boosts of confidence: 'Yes, you are doing the right thing'. Those in relationships of a more permanent nature may refer more to their partners for advice. Friends can be useful sounding boards, because they are working: employers have their own, vested interests, especially if they have invested heavily in your training, and family have their own interests to safeguard. Many also seek an impartial form of help outside of friends and family. This is where the careers adviser or the life coach, and the self-help book can be very useful.

Get yourself a motivator – a close friend, perhaps the people you live with, or a partner – somebody who believes in what you are doing. We all need someone who will 'kick our butts' at the end of a busy day and tell us to get out there and study, or search yet another Web site, or focus on that CV.

> I'd never have done this course if it wasn't for my mate, John. On all those nights I wanted to watch the football, or go down the pub, he

reminded me what I was studying for and how much I hated my job. After I'd studied for an hour or two, he'd tell me to relax in front of the telly and watch the football, if it was on. You need people like that to support you, especially if your course is fairly long – mine was a year and there were many times when I wondered if it was all really worth it.

Why do people resist change?

'Don't be stupid – you could never do that!'

Sometimes when we are planning to do great things, comments from others can make us stop dead in our tracks and ask ourselves whether we are taking on more than we can chew. When you have been knocked down before, you learn to get back up again to continue along life's path. People handle change in different ways. Some are extremely set in their routines and find change disturbing, threatening, something to be avoided at all costs. Others welcome it. Much depends on personality – and how much a person is aware of change itself. Often the people who greet our ideas about changing career with the most suspicion and least enthusiasm are those who fear change, dislike disrupted routine, worry about how it might affect them and simply do not understand how the work-place is changing. Change can be very threatening to those who demand a smooth sailing and are unable to cope with rough seas or turbulent skies.

Relatives who are completely against your changing career may worry about how it will affect them and their lives, whether they will have to make adjustments to cope with your change or take over responsibilities that you normally handle but will need to delegate. Will they end up with extra work to do because you are going off to change your career? How will you cope on a lower income, if that is what your change means? Will your job change affect your rela-tionship with them? What will happen if things go wrong: what should they say? Will people think you failed in your first career because you're now getting out of it? Research will pay dividends – it will mean you can reassure them as you have all the answers at your fingertips and you will be far more convincing when you tell people why you want to change career.

If you have a partner, discuss your change with them, because they will be affected as well. Sit down together and discuss your goals as a couple over the next five years. Work out what the course will do for your employment prospects and as a way to achieving those goals. Then consider how that will impact on your opportunities as a couple, not necessarily with regard to employment but financially. Look at your change as an investment for you both, a sort of insurance in the current job market. The selling point is to help them see that this will benefit you as a couple. Encourage your partner to take up their own studies, hobbies and interests; remind yourself that they have their concerns and problems too, and give them a little time to listen to them.

If you hit difficulties, be prepared to compromise on some issues (not necessarily your career change) and work things out together so that you meet halfway; listen and try to think how the other is feeling. It may simply be a matter of accepting that you want slightly different things, allowing each other the freedom to try for them, and recognizing that your relationship improves because you have such respect for each other and understand the other person's needs. Try to talk when you are not feeling stressed; the end of a long, tiring, stressful working day is hardly the time to sit down and discuss important concerns. Get away for a weekend, or a night, or an afternoon, to talk about what you want to change in your lives. If the will is there, there usually is a way to work things out so that you both get what you want. If the amount of time you spend together is seriously reduced by your career change, see if you can take longer over it; or, alternatively, try doing things together for short bursts of time, such as an hour for lunch at the weekends; or drinking a glass of wine in the evenings like a sort of date. Special times like these do not have to last for long: 30 minutes of focused, fun time together is enough.

Children generally thrive on change and should benefit from seeing mum and dad change career – an important lesson they will have to follow themselves. And remember that at the end of the day, you are the one paying the bills. Explain what it will mean to you as an individual.

Boost your finances

Ensure your money is working its hardest for you as you prepare to change career. Meet with an adviser from your bank or building society for a personal review to see if the accounts and services you are using at the moment will continue to be the most appropriate ones. Some financial products enable you to take a break from monthly mortgage payments, giving you a chance to have a breather if you need one. Find out if there are any products which improve the return on your savings, or to help you to save more money as you prepare to change career.

Banks, building societies and independent financial advisers may offer products, services, information and advice if you want to run your own business or franchise; they can provide advice for students, along with help on pensions, health insurance, mortgages and loans for retraining.

Many financial products now offer breaks from paying premiums, especially for those who have been made redundant or who are changing jobs. This means that for a while you can stop making payments and resume them when you are ready. Don't feel as though you should have any particular loyalty to one bank or building society; shop around until you find one offering you advice and a service you feel comfortable with, and don't make any hasty decisions.

NEXT STEP
Strengthen your financial position.

Have you:

Cleared your credit card debts and any overdraft (even if this means cutting down on your social life – good friends will understand).

Yes/No

Cut up your credit cards and store cards. Keep one card only for emergencies – the one with the best rate of interest.

Yes/No

Started saving. Put some money aside every month until you have enough to last at least three months without a job if you are planning to have time out.

Yes/No

Got things done which are going to be costly to the house, the car, your wardrobe.

Yes/No

You can cut down costs by taking up hobbies and interests that are not expensive, eg walking, cycling, reading, attending adult education classes, and by shopping locally as opposed to visiting the supermarket – we cut our food bills by 33 per cent by doing this and it took no longer, was far more relaxing and far more sociable.

You should also consider:

- How would you cope if you are not on a fixed mortgage and the interest rate goes up?
- What financial reserves have you?
- What emergencies might you have to cope with, eg family illness (include pets)?
- What insurance have you got to cover unemployment, sickness, etc?
- What are you doing to prepare for retirement?
- Are your savings tax efficient?

Perhaps you could boost your savings by opening a 'Career change' bank account, dedicated to saving money to help you change career by buying the right wardrobe, networking, studying and training (of course, you may decide to take out a bank loan instead).

137

Maintain your focus

Top Tip

Be persistent.
Do not give up when things go wrong.
If you really want to change badly enough, you will keep trying.

If you can show an employer how you have managed your life and career change, you will enhance your ability to sell yourself and to prove your commitment to your new working life. The people who fail are those who give up early. Be persistent.

Summary exercises: turn your ideas into reality and change your career

1. Work out when in the week you are going to allocate time to your career change.

2. Share your thoughts with friends or partners to see if they can add fresh insight to the way you're organizing your life.

Top Tip

Look ahead.
Allow yourself to get excited.
You are on your way to a new adventure and a new life.

---

8 Boosting your skills base and closing your knowledge gaps

Although transferable skills enable us to hit the ground running in new roles far more quickly, they will not be sufficient on their own to 'get in' to a new career and make the transition. In fact, they can lull us into a sense of false security. You need to adopt a businesslike, four-pronged approach to achieve the outcome you want – a career change:

- Training/study – to acquire specialist knowledge relevant to your new career, unless your new career happens to be a serious hobby you have participated in all your life; you may also need to acquire new skills. Finding the right course for you is important.

- Learning – to absorb the culture so that you start to talk the same language; brushing up on your job-hunting skills, because what works in one sector will not necessarily do so in another.

- Voluntary efforts – to show you can relate to the people you'll be working with.

- Networking – to raise your profile amongst the network of people who work in the sector.

NEXT STEP

Train and study for that new career.

The point to start with here is that *you are not alone*. Adults all over the country are preparing to change career. As I have stressed earlier, *whatever* you did before, the likelihood is that you will need to get training to change career, full-time or part-time in the classroom, on the job, distance learning or at home online. Remember that mature students (that's you, over 21), do not necessarily have to meet the same strict entry requirements demanded of the 16 to 21-year-old age group. You are longer in the tooth, you have more experience of life and you have a greater idea of where you are headed. Readers who left school at 14 or 15 without qualifications might be interested to hear of Access courses, fast-track learning designed for mature students as a one-year route into degree programmes. If you are reading this over a glass of wine thinking, 'Great – that's just what I'm looking for!', visit www.ucas.ac.uk/access for details of courses. In the weightier courses, like medicine and veterinary science which are very scientific, you may still find you have to go back to the traditional A-level entry requirements – there are no short cuts.

Mature students do not necessarily have to stick to the strict entry requirements demanded of 18-year-olds. Admissions tutors want most of all to make sure that your brain is working and your study habits are up to speed. They welcome the commitment and understand the risks mature students are taking to study, particularly on a full-time basis. What they will especially want to see is evidence of recent ability for you to study at an advanced level, perhaps at night school. A system known as the Accreditation of Prior Learning (APL) can save you months or even a year or so on the training rung. APL was devised on the basis that re-learning what people actually already know through past experience is a waste of time. It is far better to establish what you know and use that as a starting point from which to boost your knowledge. Course tutors will assess your past experience, skills and knowledge to see how they may contribute to the course you want to study, so they can lead to exemptions. Additionally, you may have studied units of degree courses at other universities which may, if they are part of the credit accumulation transfer scheme, contribute towards a degree course. Some degrees (but not all) lead to exemptions from the early stages of professional examinations, but you need to check that this is the case with your course tutor.

ASK YOURSELF
How can I best ensure that the course I'm going to follow will lead to a job?

Nothing in life is guaranteed, and no course will promise you a job at the end of it. But you can try to gauge how effective a course is in preparing people for a job by asking questions such as:

- What am I doing this for?
- What do I want to get out of it?
- What are the components of the course? Can I see myself enjoying studying them?
- What do employers think of this qualification?
- What sort of practical support can I expect from my family and employers?
- Who can I talk to who has done the course and obtained the sort of job I want after it?
- Where have past students gone after doing the course?
- What will it cost me? Tuition fees? Exam fees? Equipment?
- How relevant is this course to my career plans? Does it offer me the chance to have hands-on experience? Will I be able to put theory into practice? How will it increase my chances of getting the career I want?
- Who is teaching the course? How in touch are they with what is happening in this sector? What is their network of contacts like?
- Does the course include a period of work experience?
- How many hours a week will I need to devote to studying to be successful? How will I fit these into my life?
- What outcomes and expectations of the students do tutors have? Are they alert to my goals to get a job, and what help can I expect from them and the training provider to achieve this goal?
- Does the course focus on the future? Will it offer practical advice on job hunting or setting up my own business

afterwards? Can I get advice from a careers counsellor at the college to plan my next step?

- Can I get any credit for the things I have done in the past which will mean I can short-cut the length of the course through my past experiences and knowledge (ie APL)?
- Will the course lead to any exemptions from professional exams?
- How is the course assessed and delivered? Will that method suit me?
- Over what timescale is this course delivered? Can I study it on a full-time, part-time, distance-learning or e-learning basis?
- Who assesses this course for quality? Is it accredited?
- Will this course grant me exemptions from any further exams I might want to take?

You should also ascertain if any previous study and experience will count towards any courses you have done previously, under schemes such as the Credit Accumulation Transfer System and the Accreditation of Prior Learning and Experience.

'How can I fund this training and study?'

Career development loans There are deferred repayment bank loans which help you pay for vocational education or training specifically aimed to a particular job, on a full-time, part-time or distance-learning basis. They are offered through Barclays, the Co-operative and the Royal Bank of Scotland (you do not have to be an account holder with these banks). They provide between £300 and £8,000 to help you fund up to two years of training (three if the course includes work experience). You pay the loan back to the bank over an agreed period at a fixed rate of interest. Check with your local education authority with regard to career development loans to see if any funding is likely to be forthcoming and work out how you would survive on the money you would have.

Student loans These are available for those wishing to enter higher education, and must be repaid after your course. That is a topic that has created a considerable amount of debate, and it is particularly important to make sure you are well up to date with current developments in this area if you are going to study a higher education course.

College and university funds – such as Access funds to help those in dire financial need.

Charities and trusts funds Some universities and colleges have hardship or trust funds; you can find information on these in books such as the Charities Digest Directory of Grant-Making Trusts, and the Grant Register.

Scholarships These are rarely given by universities – or companies.

Bursaries – eg NHS Bursaries which may be means-tested, to help you with living expenses from one day to the next.

Employment-based training Some employers will take people on and train them at the same time, often on a sort of conveyor belt process so that they always have a number of people coming through the system.

Savings Your own savings.

Personal loans Taking out a personal loan with a financial services company.

Top Tip

Check with the college, university or training provider
to find out exactly what the application process is.
For higher education courses, for example, you can now apply
online.

'Where can I get a reference from, if I'm going to be a mature student?'

If you have been out of education for a long time, admissions tutors will want to see evidence of recent serious academic study, such as an Access course, or A level course at night school or by correspondence college. In this case, you can ask your tutor to act as a referee. Alternatively, ask someone who is a professionally qualified person or a manager to provide a reference. Check with the course Admissions Tutors for further advice.

Be prepared to put the 'legwork' in

Work out the best place for you to study, and the best time; for example, some people are fresher in the morning, getting up an hour earlier than usual (it is amazing how you can get used to this), or after the children have gone to bed. Schedule your learning time into the part of your day when disruption is least likely. Studying in the early morning does have its advantages:

- the phone is less likely to ring – a particularly useful thing if your house is full of teenagers;
- you will feel refreshed and more positive;
- your brain is not bogged down from the hassles of the day;
- you will arrive at work knowing you have already done something to hasten your way out of a job you do not enjoy doing any more – you have already done something for 'you'.

Survival tips for studying

1. Work out what you need to do in advance, so that you can plan your study time and you know what you need to complete when.
2. Build in time to allow for flexibility, in case of family illnesses, work commitments, an unexpected opportunity to enjoy yourself, so that you do not miss course deadlines.
3. Do not be afraid to ask for help if problems arise which interfere with your studies, do not wait until they have developed to such an extent that they are insurmountable.

4. Try to study a little every day with one day off, whether it is half an hour one night, three hours another. Do not let everything build up all at once. This is an excellent way to avoid unnecessary stress.
5. Seek support from other students. You are all battling to make the best use of the time available to you. You will get considerable benefit from talking and sharing ideas together:

We sat down to do the assignment at one person's home, and realized we were brain dead. It was a Thursday night, most of us had worked a horrendously long week, and we were all exhausted. Not one of us had a single original thought to offer. To lighten the atmosphere, we cracked open some beers and a bottle of wine, and talked about other things for a bit. When we went back to the assignment later, our thoughts were really flowing. Within an hour, we had the outline of the project cracked.

Remember, adult education is very different from that you may recall in your schooldays, and your tutors will be well versed in handling students with family problems, work hassles, and the other worries and commitments adulthood brings. The important thing is not to let these problems fester and think you can handle them. *Keep people informed and do not give them any surprises.* They will be far more cooperative and understanding of your situation if you are upfront (but not aggressive) from the start.

'Short courses can be really useful.'

If running your own business is your aim, you will discover many colleges run courses on this subject. They also run some useful evening classes concerned with promoting yourself, dress sense, giving presentations, public speaking, assertiveness training and working with the press, along with the inevitable stream of IT courses on offer. Make use of them all where you can if you feel your skills in these areas need boosting. You never know who you will meet, apart from anything else – people who could be useful future contacts.

NEXT STEP

Boost your knowledge about what is happening in the sector.

If at the same time as making and developing contacts you can prove your seriousness by showing your interest in what is happening in their world, so much the better. Talk to your contacts about any courses you are undertaking, articles you may have read, and ask questions that show interest and that you are thinking about the way their sector is going. Try to get involved where you are going to meet people who are going to have contacts they can refer you to.

Read the relevant trade magazines, and check out the professional body's Web sites regularly. Be ready to comment on any articles you've seen in the press about the sector.

Employers do not like taking on 'risks' so the more you have done in their field to show that you are the right choice, the better. The more people you have talked to, the more you have investigated their sector and learnt their language, and can show you know about the big and small names in it, the better for you. Think through the major issues facing the industry and try to spot opportunities for growth.

NEXT STEP

Aim to boost the skills and knowledge you'll need and the ability to hit the ground running by showing what you can do via voluntary efforts.

Prepare to hit the ground running in your new career and charge up the right skills. You may be able to do this while you are in your current job, preparing for your career change, unbeknown to your boss. Spice up your job – get some responsibilities under your belt at work which offer you the opportunity to develop skills you are going to need in your new line of work. Can you volunteer to take on a project which would give you the chance to develop skills you would need in your new career and give you the opportunity to achieve something? Take any opportunity you can wherever you get the chance while you are in your current job to increase your chances of getting out, by building skills you will need for your new career (your employer need never know why you have really volunteered...)

Get out there and show you can relate to the people and to the tasks you will be dealing with. Experience doesn't necessarily equal paid work. You can acquire it voluntarily, at the weekends, or, if your proposed career relates to a hobby, at night via evening class or simply by doing the hobby, eg writing, photography, craft work, catering – all relate to possible careers. They can provide both a way to boost your skills and to meet people from a wide range of backgrounds. They are always keen to take volunteers on board and they may provide the perfect chance for you to develop your skills. Examples include:

- charities;
- committee work;
- environment organizations;
- local zoos;
- homes for the elderly and sick;
- local schools;
- churches;
- political parties;
- arts centres;
- hospital radio stations;
- conservation societies.

They may all provide opportunities for you to develop skills in customer care, selling, promoting, publicizing, fund-raising, counselling, developing people, designing logos, interviewing, advising, entertaining, planning, organizing, and checking. And all will be glad of helpers. For more information, visit the Web site for the National Centre for Volunteering at www.volunteering.org.uk. You can also visit www.csv.org.uk for opportunities in the UK and Europe; and if you really want to have a complete change and go abroad, try www.vso.org.uk and take off for a couple of years. Track the skills you are using and the experience you are gaining; any achievements and new contacts; and think carefully about what you are learning and observing.

NEXT STEP

Get insight into the career you'll be going into if you can, and try to get some work experience.
Potential employers are always impressed by people who've given up their time for free, or had to go through some material hardship, such as paying to do a course. It shows you're serious about what you're doing. And if one employer can't help you get a starting foothold in the door, try another.

Top Tip

Use some of your holiday allowance from your current job to spend time getting an insight into your chosen career. The time you spend will pay dividends.

Key questions to ask yourself include:

- What do I want to get out of this exercise? What do I want to learn?
- Who are the key people I'll learn from?
- How far can I expect to expand my network of contacts who might be able to help me later on?
- What can I bring to benefit this organization?

This last point is important, because although you may not realize it, many employers benefit from outsiders coming in to their environments. If you're asking questions about the way people do things, they are likely to ask themselves, 'Well, why do I do it that way?' It makes them think about what they're doing, how they're doing it, and why. Often outsiders bring with them a new idea of how things can be done, or offer fresh insight (obviously without giving their own trade secrets away).

There may be some small project you can offer to do to 'get your hands dirty', to prove interest, show what you can do and see how you fare. In many sectors, it's what employers will expect of young people, so there's no reason why you should be any different. Both

148

you and the employer you're with will benefit from such an exercise, even if you have to do it for free. Remember, if you really want to change career, you need to go the extra mile to get a foot in the door to show you're serious about the change. You need to lessen the quantity of the unknown and risk, both from your point of view – 'Is this career really for me?' – and from prospective employers – 'Is this person really serious about this career change, or is he/she going to go back to what he/she was doing in a few months' time, which means we'll have to recruit again?'

'Can I get some paid work experience under my belt so that at least I've got something to talk about?'

If you're working while preparing for your career change, and your contract of employment permits it, then you may be able to take on some paid employment just to get your foot in the door. This could be for just a few hours a week. There are plenty of careers you can get started on so long as you stick to doing just a few small tasks to the best of your ability. Remember, you want to cultivate contacts among people who get to know your work and will tell others what a great job you're doing.

NEXT STEP

Use your network.

Contacts are everything in landing the work you want. Some 70 per cent of jobs are not advertised and often employers wait until the right people come along to fill the posts they want with the sort of people they know will do a good job. Network as widely as you can to boost your chances of hearing not only about opportunities, ie situations vacant, but also about work that needs doing – ie a project. Recruiting is expensive in terms of time and money, and it will not necessarily guarantee the job is filled successfully. Many job offers will appear through personal recommendations. Do not forget that people are under too much pressure to want to spend hours recruiting staff, especially for short-term needs. Get about, and network, make contacts, offer help. Ask what the best way 'in' is for career changers such as yourself. Being in the right place at the right time can secure exactly the job you want, be it on a free-lance or 'permanent' staff basis. You want to get talking to as many people as possible in the sector so that, when people are talking amongst themselves about their recruitment needs, your name pops up into conversation. Employers would far rather recruit somebody who has been recommended to them who has shown enthusiasm, initiative, commitment and dedication in pursuing a career they really want, so far as their current jobs will allow.

'Who do I know who can help me get a foot in the door?'

Create your own network. Write down all the people you know and the jobs or careers they hold. Your list will amaze you.

Networking contacts

Friends of the family	Your own friends
Relatives	Members of clubs you belong to
Professional organizations	Local business people you use yourself
People you meet through hobbies/interests	Community workers
Employers you meet	Relatives/friends' current employers
Guidance and course tutors	Careers services
Job centres	The church
Chat rooms in the right kind of Web site	People you know living abroad
Press articles on a company quoting a name	Company Web sites giving names of people to contact

Retraining programmes	Advertisements in the press with names on them

Your network could provide some of the following:

- information about the day-to-day job itself;
- names of people who might be able to help you in terms of giving you advice or tip you off about who is recruiting;
- an idea of the skills, qualities and experience the employer wants;
- an idea of whether you would be a good 'fit' into the organization;
- the names of people in charge of a particular area such as marketing, human resources, IT – all useful people to approach as they know what they are looking for;
- suggestions of firms who might be able to help you;
- advice on your CV;
- the best way to approach their company for work.

Do not feel embarrassed about using friends and family as a network. Networking can pay dividends, not only for you in gaining your employment, but for them. Many companies now pay staff who recommend people as prospective recruits who are later taken on. Nor can people do it for just the money. If things go wrong and those they recommend leave, then that reflects badly on them and their judgement.

Aim to expand your network of contacts all the time, and not just when you are looking for work. Raise your profile locally so you get known – and offer to do something for the people you meet – to extend your network of contacts and increase your knowledge and understanding of the sector. Join professional organizations and attend local events such as job fairs, network at trade shows and trade fairs, so that you can find the right people to approach. Ask 'Who else can I talk to?' and mix with people who work in the sector you want to work in, to pick up the language, advice on getting in, your knowledge of people who are willing to help you, find out what dress works, where they socialize etc.

As you make contacts, tell people of your intentions to get into their sector and talk to them about your past achievements, – briefly, to give them an idea of what you are made of. If you are lucky, people will say more than, 'I wish you luck'. They may add, 'Well, when you are ready to look for work, let me know – we could use somebody like you'. Try to link your past achievements with things they might want to achieve so that you can show how you might be useful to them. That said, do not rely on that one person. Times change and they may move on. Do not put all your eggs into one basket.

And finally...

When you're considering a career change and meeting people, it's important to remember that this is their chosen field. They've spent a while in their careers, and most likely worked hard to get to where they are, building up their knowledge, experience, skills and views on the sector and where it's going, especially if they're passionate about it. Enter you, an outsider, walking into their world to see if it's for you. Listen to advice people have to offer about ways 'in' so far as you are concerned, and reflect on it. Remember, this is their industry and they know what works in it. Help yourself:

- Don't think the world owes you a living and that you can just waltz into another sector and get a job. You need to work at it like anybody else. This could mean doing some work for nothing to prove your worth, or starting at the bottom and starting small, as opposed to gunning for the big names straight away.
- Always be on time – never, ever risk being late. If you're asking for somebody's help, this is particularly important.
- Dress up rather than down. When you've made it, you can take more risks on this front. Right now, work hard to create the right impression. This is the case even if you're going in for an informal chat.
- Remember that courtesy goes a long way. The people who are helping you could be thinking, 'Would we want to work with this person? Would we want him/her on our team?' A

spirit of goodwill and cooperation and thoughtfulness in busy environments is essential.

Running your own business

If you want to run your own business or franchise, you will need to follow similar lines, making particular efforts to boost your knowledge in:

- starting up a small business;
- finance and accountancy;
- marketing;
- advertising;
- handling the administrative side of things;
- developing your entrepreneurial skills.

You can do this by taking courses, or reading books that cover these sorts of areas (see Useful addresses and further information). There are also organizations designed to help the person running his or her own business. Finally, see if there is a local group you can join where you can meet people who are already running their own businesses successfully. Try to discuss the problems they meet and how they overcome them, and ask their advice generally.

Summary

1. Boost your knowledge, skills, personal profile and contacts to cultivate your chances of landing a job in your new career.
2. Be prepared for these efforts to take over much of your life – other things will need to make way for them.
3. Enjoy the feeling of achievement and direction your life has taken on as you prepare to change your career.

Summary exercises

1. Put the names of all the contacts you are making in a safe place so that you can refer to them in future. Keep in touch with them regularly to remind them of your interest. Is there anyone among your contacts who would vouch for your efforts to change career in a reference?

2. Start restructuring your CV to include things that will spark the interest of prospective employers. Make notes of what you can add under work experience, educational history, interests and referees.

9 *Sharpen your personal sales pitch*

What you are now saying is you have done your groundwork and you think 'I'm ready to go out there and pitch for work'. In part, it is also about pulling your career history together so that you can sell yourself effectively and convince employers that your life story flows and that you have managed your career, ie taken control of it.

Ground rules to sharpen your sales pitch are:

1. Always demonstrate a professional approach in your job hunting to show seriousness of mind and that you are not a time-waster.
2. Target the right people and companies.
3. Make sure that any correspondence you send out, eg CVs, letters, application forms, are perfectly presented – no grammatical errors and spelling errors. Get them checked over and keep copies to refresh your memory of your efforts prior to any meetings.
4. Use plenty of examples from your past and current activities and research to show that you are really and genuinely interested in the sector in which you are planning to work.
5. Do not be critical of your current or past employers in front of prospective employers and customers.
6. Be determined and tenacious in pursuing opportunities – do not be put off by rejections; the right job will come along.
7. Be very positive about your career change. If you don't believe in it, nobody else will.

Small, medium and large businesses all use different ways to take on staff. Find out how companies recruit staff in your proposed career, and you could save yourself a lot of time and heartbreak. The Internet is an excellent resource for this. Recruitment methods vary from one company to another within the sector, too. Many smaller companies will stick to tried and tested methods, such as using the local press, and will often follow up letters sent to them by hopeful prospective recruits. Others will use agencies and the Internet to land staff, because these save them a great deal of time and effort.

The first step to take is to prepare your job hunting tools.

NEXT STEP

Get ready to sell yourself and identify employers to approach.

This section will focus on your self-promotion kit to boost your chances of landing work. Remember, employers will be asking themselves three major questions as they view your application and meet you: can you do the job? Will you do it? And will you fit into the culture of the organization?

When you are moving into your selling mode, remind yourself of the skills, qualities and experience employers will want. Review your past life for evidence of these, either in work or through hobbies and interests.

Before you start the voyage to secure work, and put your CV and covering letter together, focus again on what you can offer. Consider the following questions and try to provide three or four bullet points per answer: think of an example you can give an employer to demonstrate each bullet point in your career – do not feel you have to restrict yourself to examples from the workplace; try to relate each bullet to anything you know you might experience in your new job, as a result of the research you have done and people you have talked to about it.

ASK YOURSELF

'What are my skills?
What can I do for this employer?'

Ultimately, what matters to a company recruiting staff is an individual's ability to do a job, his or her willingness to get it done, what he or she could achieve on the job (over and above the job description) and how he or she will 'fit' with the culture of the organization.

Look at the skills and knowledge you have got already which you would need in your proposed career. Transferable skills will show an employer that you can be effective at work. Your application will probably prove that you have the basic core skills every single person needs at work – reading, writing, basic computer literacy and basic maths. (Remember, there are many people in the UK who do not have these.)

Depending on the job you want, you will need a particular level of skill and you will need to select examples that are relevant to the job you want to do to prove you have skills:

Transferable skills	problem solving, managing yourself and your work, communicating clearly and effectively in writing and orally
Interpersonal skills	ability to get on with other people, and how to influence them appropriately depending on the career you want
Management skills	how to lead a team, motivate others, direct, delegate, supervise, plan, control, administer, reward
Strategic skills	knowledge of where you are going and how to get there

Try to think of ways you can relate examples of your transferable skills to ways in which you know you will use them in your proposed career, so that you can demonstrate to prospective employers or customers that you have the skills you need in a context and language they will relate to and understand.

A key area employers will be interested in is in your vocational and technical skills, those skills you have learnt for the purpose of your new career. Add examples of skills you have acquired previously that are related to your new career, which you know the job will demand. Where in your past life history can you show you have used these skills? Do not stick to only jobs for examples – think more broadly than that. How can you provide evidence of their effectiveness? Mention any courses you have undertaken, outlining what they covered and explaining when and how you studied them. Include here all the open learning you have done in order to take charge of your own development, such as talking to people doing the work, so that you can show you have a good idea of what it involves; and reading about the sector itself.

ASK YOURSELF

What are my strengths and weaknesses?

Describe your strengths; sit down with your best friend and ask him or her what your strengths are before relating those to how you will be able to use them at work. For example: 'I make things happen. – I will have an idea and, after appropriate consultation with those involved, I will make the idea happen'; or 'I relate well to all age groups. – I can relate to anyone coming into the business and enjoy working with a variety of people, both staff and customers'.

Look at your weaknesses. How can you handle them positively? Can you show ways in which you overcome these, perhaps by altering the way you deal with them and trying to show you have developed strategies for tackling them? We all have weaknesses, employers know that. What matters is describing to others how we are trying to overcome them.

ASK YOURSELF

What have I achieved?

Be very clear about this and spell it out. Think of something you have achieved in the last three years – anything. The following will help employers understand the scale of your achievements:

- numbers;
- budgets;
- targets;
- verbs implying action;
- using qualities to build a picture of how you work;
- team/company goals;
- money;
- business won;

- percentages;
- staffing allocation;
- policies;
- timescales;
- circumstances at that time which made your task more challenging;
- reductions;
- savings;
- positive impacts.

Typical examples of the above could include: 'I expanded the exchange scheme from 44 students participating to 88 in just three years with no extra staff and a 2 per cent dropout rate'; or 'I organized a higher education fair within budget of £5,000: 33 institutions attended, 1,700 students came through in one day; in feedback, 74 per cent said they would go on to higher education as a result of the effectiveness of the fair; plans are to expand it next year to 50 institutions'.

NEXT STEP

Prepare your CV.

There are a great many books on the market outlining how best to write a CV, and I have included a couple of them under 'Further reading' at the back of this book. Many careers and job hunting Internet Web sites also offer plenty of advice on the subject. There are a number of different ways to write a CV, and you need to find one you feel comfortable with. The guidelines are:

- Keep it short – nobody has time to read more than two pages.

- Make sure it is easy to read by using plenty of bullet points and no long paragraphs.
- Get the CV proofread. There must be no spelling or grammatical errors in it.
- Do not put the words 'CV' or 'curriculum vitae' at the top. Employers know what it is. Head it with your name.
- Be honest.

In the case of you, the career changer:

- Use a personal profile after your initial personal details (name, address and contact details including e-mail address) to give the reader an immediate impression of the sort of person you are and what you're looking for.
- Be strong on what you have achieved, not what your responsibilities are.
- Mention any courses you have done or voluntary efforts you've undertaken to equip yourself to work competently in the sector.
- Use hobbies and interests if they can provide evidence of interest in the sector and the role, or skills and qualities the post demands such as team-building.
- Remember that the job of the CV is to get you an interview, to get your foot in the door.

ASK YOURSELF

How can I best boost my chances and put myself a cut above everybody else?

In these days of a value-added culture, the prospective employers will also be asking themselves, 'What can you offer that nobody else can?' Whatever your career aspirations are, when you go out to sell yourself to an employer or customer, you will need to show how you, as an individual, can offer that 'value-added' concept, that particular something nobody else can. Many employers recruit people with experience from other backgrounds because it is their background that makes them what they are – it brings something different to the company, such as a fresh approach, a new insight or way of handling things. So ask yourself: 'What makes me unique?'

'How can I persuade anybody that I'm absolutely serious about and committed to this career change?'

An important element in any self-promotion effort is to tell the employer what you want to do and achieve within their organization. On their own, transferable skills are not going to be enough to make the jump between one career and another. Show an employer you are serious about changing career and that you plan to achieve the change by:

- being willing to train (in your own time if necessary);
- having prepared for your new career by undertaking training and study already;
- acquiring what experience you can so that you will be able to hit the ground running when you start;
- being able to give the names of people as referees, with whom they are acquainted, who can vouch for your efforts and seriousness;
- acquiring work – even on a short-term basis;
- showing what you've done to research your career so that you're sure you're moving in the right direction, and being ready to explain where the idea for your new career came from;
- making sure your image is right for your new career.

Try to show that you are up to date with trends and developments in the sector in which you want to work. At the letter of application stage, this may mean describing the research you have done, not just about the career itself but about the sector. You might refer to people you have talked to about such a move; or a recent article you have just read in a trade or business publication; or a reference to something the company has done or is doing – and sell your background as something that can only benefit your future employer. Use examples of your transferable skills to show how you can bring about change or contribute to make things happen and fit in with the company's culture – however large or small. It is simply a matter of using the right examples.

'How can I tackle the age thing?'

Some sectors tend to recruit younger people because of the image they want to portray. If this is the case in the sector in which you want to work, try to portray youthful characteristics in your CV.

Have you:	**Yes/No**
shown you are able to mix with people of all ages (but do not mention your own children in your CV) and how this might fit in with the employer's public image?	_____
explained how comfortable you are with IT and described the applications you are proficient in?	_____
shown that you are able and willing to adapt to change and that you are not 'fixed' in your ideas, by giving examples of keeping up with developments and trends in your sector?	_____
talked in terms of long-term plans in the sector to show you will be worth investing in?	_____
looked to apply to companies where your image will fit?	_____

Finally, why not visit Web sites such as www.agepositive.gov.uk, which is packed with useful case studies.

> ## NEXT STEP
> ### Prepare for contact with prospective employers.

- Set up your own Internet address – don't use the one at work, as employers snoop. If you don't have access to the Net at home, use an Internet café/shop or public library.
- Give out your mobile number and home telephone number and address to people you're talking to about your change, but not your direct line at work. If an agency or prospective employer calls and you can't talk because you're surrounded by your colleagues, simply say, 'It's not a good moment to talk right now. Can I call you back later?' and get a number and time to telephone them.
- Keep your goals private at work. They may take a while to achieve and you'll need to keep the cash coming in, pay off debts and try to build up some savings as you go.

> ## NEXT STEP
> ### Use your network to secure work.

There are many methods to job hunt, but you should remember that some 70 per cent of jobs aren't advertised at all – the process is costly in terms of time and money. As a career changer, you may need to be particularly creative in finding work, and one of the first things you can do is to let people know you're out there and hunting. If you've done your research properly, acquired a network of contacts, and sold yourself effectively as a serious career changer, you'll find it's just a matter of being in the right place and the right time when it comes to landing that great job. People often find work as a result of just talking to others about what they're doing. But be persistent – perseverance pays.

Look back to Chapter 8 and remind yourself of the network you have developed over the years and, in particular, since you started the journey to change your career. Now is the time to get in touch with all your contacts and find out if they know of anybody who is recruiting. If you can be flexible, and short term project work is an option as opposed to being 'permanent', that will increase your chances of landing employment and getting stuck in. Remind contacts how they helped you and then show what you have done to further your career plans since you last met or talked – it is helpful to send a copy of your CV so that they have a good idea of your background. See if they have any further suggestions to make. Always thank them for any help they give you and never be pushy or demanding.

Go to the heart of the sector, where people meet and talk, to raise your profile

If you can gain access to an organization, either by doing voluntary work, or temping, you'll have an opportunity to make yourself known and valued, and someone they will not want to lose; your chances of landing employment will be greatly enhanced.

You may have to expand your goals for a while at the same time gaining training and experience, in order to make the move into the area you really want to be in. For example, if you wanted to work in a university library, but there was no university in your town, you might think about applying to further education colleges in the area, or your local library to at least start picking up the right sort of skills and experience. At least you will be in the right sort of sector.

Contacting companies directly

Don't limit your thoughts only to the FTSE companies here. I am referring to the small company employing 20 people, just as much as the blue chip organizations who have thousands of staff worldwide. If you want to write to an employer on spec, visit their Web site to see if you can obtain any names of people to write to, preferably the person in charge of the section you want to work for, or ring up to find out who you can write to. You can visit company Web sites and check out their careers or jobs or recruitment pages, and e-mail your CV to them in order to express your interest; or you can do the same thing by post. It is useful to have an angle to 'hook' your speculative letter onto, something you can refer to which you read in the press – 'I saw in *The Times* last Thursday that your company was...'. Read regular professional newsletters, journals and periodicals and specialist magazines relating to the field and look out for articles referring to the organization. Don't forget to check organizations' Web sites for the 'news' or 'press release' page, which can give you a fairly rapid overview of what the company has been doing. You might see an article explaining how a company is expanding, or offering a new product or service, or going to a new location; they may have won a major contract; all these things may require an extra safe pair of hands. If this is the case, write with your CV showing you have read about this new development in the paper and try to encourage them to invite you in for an interview. Even if you do not see jobs advertised, you will identify employers in your area whom you can perhaps make contact with.

Even just paying more attention to your local paper could give you ideas or point to people who need to take on extra staff. Stories about local companies could point to new opportunities and be a good time to send your CVs, referring to what you have read, or seen, or heard.

'My friend sent off 50 letters with her CV to employers. She only got 12 responses and they were all negative. What is the point of doing a spec letter?'

Many people send off a CV and letter to between 50 and 100 companies and then wonder why they do not get anywhere (even so much as a response). Companies like to feel you have written to them because they mean something to you. Employers can tell a regurgitated CV and covering letter which has gone to many other companies a mile off. It shows lack of thought, lack of focus and a half-hearted attempt to land a job. Do not waste your time and postage doing the same thing. Target organizations to go for and focus on them.

Responding to adverts on the Internet

Using the Internet can be a very rapid way to secure an interview, even over the telephone. You can register your CV with companies, recruitment agencies and Web pages devoted to employment and have vacancies e-mailed to you directly. If you are surfing the Internet for that dream job, and you are surfing the pages of a recruitment agency or job search site, most Web pages will give you the ability to search for jobs by:

- sector;
- location (within a given part of the world, country, region or town);
- salary requirements;
- preferred starting date;
- length of assignment or job;
- recent jobs.

Once the Web site has produced the jobs that are relevant to your needs, then they may tell you a bit about the company, which is often revealing if you look between the lines: the sort of role they wish to fill, and the kind of person they want to fill it.

Many sites do not give that many details about vacancies, and you are more likely to find only the briefest of job descriptions, with very basic requirements of what the post demands and the sort of person they are looking for. Why not e-mail the company with a few carefully thought-out questions, not just about the role they have advertised, but about the direction of the company itself, or pull the phone number and a name off the site and call them to have a brief chat? Are there any employee profiles on the Web sites? Have any of them changed career before starting with the company?

'I've been reading adverts on the Internet and in the press. How can you learn anything from so little information?'

Let us study one advert for a recruitment consultant in a town in the south of England in more detail: It was on the Internet, but it could have been in the local press, too. The following are amongst some of the requirements the advert says the company wants.

'A willingness to achieve and beat daily and weekly targets.'

This should give you an idea of the pressure that will be put on the new recruit, because there are weekly *and* daily targets, which means you will always be conscious that you have to perform throughout the entire week. Can you show that you have survived under that sort of pressure and, indeed, that you relish that sort of challenge? (One of your questions at interview could be to find out who sets the targets and whether they are enforced on staff or agreed with them.)

'Experience in the recruitment industry is not essential.'

If you have recruited staff at all before, you have an insight into what the client – the employer using the agency to recruit his staff – is going through and might expect. As with any vacancy, if you do not have something they would prefer, but you can meet all the other requirements, try to develop a strategy for overcoming the areas where you are lacking. Can you comment on your experiences or refer to trends and issues the industry is facing throughout your application? Can you talk about experiences you have had of recruitment agencies as an applicant and show that you have thought about what people seeking work want as they come through the door? Show that you have done your homework in terms of finding out as much about the recruitment industry as you can by referring to articles you have read in the press, discussions you have had with recruitment and human resource professionals, small business advisers, company personnel... at the very least, show you are aware of the strengths, weaknesses, threats and opportunities facing the industry.

'You must have an excellent telephone manner and be comfortable speaking to people face to face or on the telephone.'

Can you show how your research has given you an insight into the day-to-day work of a recruitment consultant – handling enquiries from employers and applicants and dealing with people who feel pressured?

If the advert specifies that applicants must have very particular skills that you do not posess, then your wisest route is to find a way to acquire those before you respond to any such advert. Some companies are willing to train people up to a certain level of competency, but not all.

'A flexible schedule is necessary.'

This is likely to mean that the job comes first, and your personal life second. Consider what you wanted in terms of the work–life balance. If you have found work that you enjoy so much that you feel you could work 20 hours a day if necessary, so be it. But just check with yourself: is that what your career change was all about? How far will the 'flexible schedule' interfere with your life? Will it mean cancelling your holidays at the last minute because of a new contract won by the company? Or simply that you cancel your aerobics class because you have to stay late to prepare for an impromptu meeting the following morning?

The Web page or advert will tell you how to respond and, whatever you do, follow the instructions to the letter. If the advert tells you to e-mail your CV to somebody, do precisely that, accompanied by a few short sentences that explain where you saw the advert, what appeals about it and what you are seeking to do. If you are responding by e-mail, you can either include your CV within the body of your message or as an attachment. It goes without saying that if a reference number is quoted, you should mention it. Apart from anything else, it shows a professional approach and attention to detail.

NEXT STEP

If appropriate, sign up with recruitment agencies.

Signing up with recruitment agencies

There are increasing numbers of specialist agencies and firms taking on temporary staff to help out with increased workloads such as a new contract, a project that needs to be done, as well as the traditional cover for maternity leave, sickness and holidays. From this point of view, agencies can be useful in terms of getting you out there to start building up experience. If you are going to an agency in person, go armed with your CV and a flexible, enthusiastic but determined approach. You can work through an agency by going online, so you can register, send your CV and look at the jobs available. Agencies may offer you the opportunity to boost your skills through training, give advice on careers and CV writing, often for free, such as www.reed.co.uk or www.stepstone.co.uk.

While you are waiting for that permanent job to land at your feet, agencies can be useful in terms of offering you short-term or temporary work while you are finding a longer term position. These sorts of positions can be invaluable ways to show what you can do and get a reputation as somebody who would be great to have on board. Temping can be a very helpful way to achieve a career change because it can buy you time and keep the money coming in. In some areas it will provide you with a really useful foot in the door. Talk to people about your skills and ambitions and show an interest. Whatever sector you are in, the 'temp-to-perm' route gives everybody a chance to see if the relationship between organization and individual is going to work, from both sides. Temping will increase your ability to be flexible, to sell yourself and to adapt to changing circumstances – three useful skills in today's workplace. It will also enhance your confidence in your own competency and abilities. You will develop an ability to think globally and locally because of the different organizations you work for, and a strong network of contacts. You can also develop assignments to fit in with your own career goals so that you have the time to achieve them.

Be flexible

Think creatively about the ways 'in' to a company. How can you get a foot in the door? You could try going under it, ie taking a low-level position and working your way up to the job you want, proving yourself as you go and taking on extra projects to make sure your career moves in the direction you want. Bear in mind that you may need to take a drop in salary. It is proof of your interest and you will probably find that, although a struggle, life will have greater happiness for you in future.

Think ahead. Could the job you are offered give you the chance to get experience and make further contacts in a field to prove your interest? How might the organization change in the future? Could you use the job as an opportunity to get in there and mould it to the sort of work you had in mind?

Using traditional methods

One of the most popular methods of job hunting is to browse the papers for vacancies that may interest you. There are pros and cons: the jobs advertised in the local (and national) paper may give you an idea of what is around in your area, and nationally, and you will obtain useful advice about job-hunting skills in columns. You will also get a good idea of who is responsible for recruiting in which firm – although approaching the human resources department is not usually the most effective way to get an interview. The problem with this method is that thousands of other people will have seen the advertisement and you will need to ensure that you make yourself really stand out from the crowd. Understandably, many of them will not be completely right for the job. They will not send in beautifully presented CVs or think about what the employer wants; but a great many will.

If you are downsizing your career and looking for lower level work, consider visiting the job centre and checking shop windows and noticeboards in the supermarket, the bank and the post office. Most of the vacancies advertised by the latter are fairly local, low-level stuff, but if your main motivation to work is to give you something that enables you to rush home at lunchtime to let the dog out, they may provide an answer to your employment problems and, at the same time, give you the satisfaction that you are contributing to community life. And, in fact, studying such vacancies may give you an idea for your own business. UK employment services are offering all job centre vacancies – plus advice – on their site at www.jobcentreplus.gov.uk.

Find out if there are any flexible routes or employment-based training tracks available in your area – your local job centre or careers service will be able to help you, or you can contact the regional professional body. Some training programmes can help you make contact with employers who are looking to recruit; there is nothing like being right on the spot when people are looking to take staff on. Successive governments have introduced a number of initiatives to help people retrain, such as New Deal; you can find details of these schemes at your local job centre or visit www.newdeal.gov.uk.

NEXT STEP

**Research the company you're applying to
thoroughly. Research its competitors too.**

Good preparation when applying for a job or enquiring about
possible opportunities is essential. Companies like to know why you
have targeted them, whether you want to be an employee or have
them as a client for your own business. Show you are well informed
about the organization you want to join and the sector it operates in.

Have you:	**Yes/No**
read the Annual Report	_____
visited any showrooms	_____
visited their Web site	_____
talked with people who work there	_____
searched for any details about the company in the local and national press	_____
read any company literature produced for the benefit of the shareholder or customer	_____
identified the competitors in the market and how your prospective employer's customer segment is different	_____
worked out what sort of image they want to portray and how you would fit into that image?	_____

Preparing for interviews

Before you attend any interviews with a company, visit their Web site (no excuses for not at least checking they have one, and if you are unable to find it, obtain some of their paper-based literature, which will certainly have a Web address on it). Perform a broader search to see if the company has featured in any particular press releases, so that you can comment on your research when you have an opportunity at the interview.

Interviews provide both candidate and employer with an opportunity to gather information about each other, and to gauge how well they might work together. Nerve-racking and butterfly-inducing as interviews are, you should try to think of them as a two-way process: both sides obviously have much to gain from the successful interview. Try for a minute to think of the interview from an employer's point of view: if they choose the wrong person for the job, this decision could prove to be an expensive mistake. Recruiting staff at any level costs time and money. As well as wanting to recruit someone with the right skills, softer overtones like attitude, values and personality are important in finding people who will 'fit' in with others working for the organization. Try to portray a positive picture of yourself and learn as much about the team you will be working for as you can. If possible, meet as many of them as you can, if not on the day of the interviews themselves, then certainly before you accept an offer.

Interviews are stressful, so try to think about questions you might be asked – and some you can ask yourself. It is not a good idea to ask questions about likely salary and perks – try to show a more deep-rooted interest and ask about where the company is headed, opportunities for training and development for employees and so forth. Other important items to consider include:

- Prepare your interview outfit. Dress up, rather than down, but don't go in a suit if you know that smart–casual is the norm. Pay attention to detail – clean your shoes, don't go overboard on jewellery.
- Think about your strengths and how they might be useful to your future employer.

- Review past achievements and pick out those that demonstrate the skills you will need for this job and the direct effect your contribution had.
- Be able to demonstrate flexibility and the capability to adjust to different cultures and differing circumstances.
- There is absolutely no excuse for not visiting the company's Web site. Your earlier research on the company will prepare you for questions and enable you to give informed answers that will show you have done your homework.
- Even if you are just invited in for a simple chat, assume it will be on an interview basis.

You can ask questions such as:

- Is the company going through any major changes at the moment and how will that impact on my role? How are the employees reacting towards it and what is the company doing to help them cope?
- Does the company have a statement of values?
- What is morale like in the organization, and within the team I will be working with?
- What is the team I will be working with like?
- What is the management style of my superiors?
- Will I have a mentor or coach offering me support and practical advice and guidance when I start?
- How is the company structured? Is there an organization chart I can look at?
- What is the company's position on training and development?

Try to follow up the interview with an e-mail or correspondence, thanking the interviewer for his/her time and commenting on a particular aspect of the discussion.

At the end of the day, you are looking at a two-way process. Try to get an idea of the sort of team you will be joining. The interviewers will certainly be assessing how you will fit in with the team. Will you present the company in the right light? Will you be happy at the company? Does it leave you feeling you want to go there every working day? Be prepared to think on the spot, both in answering and asking questions, and always keep the dialogue relevant.

Moving on

Don't resign from your present job unless you have:

- another one to go to;
- something constructive to do which relates to your chosen career, ie a course and you know how you are going to fund it;
- built up some savings behind you to cushion those early months when your starting salary or wage might be lower or, worse, sporadic and unreliable.

Nor should you advertise your intentions, even with trusted colleagues. You may be sticking around with your present company for some time to come, despite your desire to get out and leave them all to it. It's not a wise move to use lunch hours or quiet moments when you think nobody is looking to surf the net for jobs; most companies have checks on this area and will pick up your search straight away. Try not to change your behaviour – except to make better use of your time – and act as if nothing were happening and you are eagerly looking forward to next year's Christmas party as much as everybody else.

What is stopping you?

At this point, as you implement your strategy to change career, you may sometimes think you are not progressing as quickly as you should. Review your action plan and remind yourself of all the positive steps you have taken on this journey and how far you have come since you first actively thought of changing career. Consider your focus and attitude. We all slip up sometimes. Are you guilty of any of the following?

	Yes/No
Crises you have invented to slow down the process	_____

Procrastinating on important decisions
and taking action   _____

An inability to say no to requests for
your time and help   _____

A feeling that this is all too much effort,
you are comfortable as you are   _____

A lack of focus... you are wandering
off track   _____

It is easier to get on with other things in
your life than changing career   _____

'I'll just watch this, then I'll get stuck in'   _____

Filling up your life with trivia so you can
pretend you are 'too busy to change
career... next year, maybe'   _____

Fear of failure to achieve the change   _____

If you answer NO to most of them, you are on the track to land the job you really want. Be determined to succeed. If you answer mainly YES, ask yourself whether your desire to change career is still as strong as it was. If it is, then take action to remove the barriers that are slowing your progress and go for it. Realize your dreams and your vision!

'It seems to be taking me forever to land the job I want! Any advice?'

Keep trying. Talk to people in the sector to find out what you could do to increase your marketability and chances of being employed. See if you can go for a more flexible approach in terms of the sort of work you want. Ask if there are any projects you can do on a short-term basis. Boost your knowledge through continued reading and see if there are any other courses you can take.

Changing your career may take a few weeks or a few years, depending on the qualifications and experience you have behind you, how tremendous the change you are seeking to make is, and the level of work you want. Many changes involve using sideways moves to acquire the right angle of experience or training. Could you, for example, start manoeuvring your efforts at work so that they take you into an area that interests you?

Be patient. The length of time it takes to find a job will depend on how much effort you really honestly put into finding one; if you hope that by scanning the papers a couple of times a week you will land the job of your dreams, you might also hope to win the lottery. Spend as much time searching for that perfect job and cultivating your chances as you would if you were working. If you have a strong skills set, that will certainly help your cause. Finally, your attitude and flexibility as to the location and sort of job you want will help ease the process along considerably. Embrace lifelong learning as a personal mission, rather than leaving it to government pamphlets. Think laterally, deliberately look to apply your skills and experience, values and interests to as wide a section of employment opportunities as you can.

This may be the low point, especially if you find yourself taking a huge step backwards by leaving your past job and perhaps going out to do some short-term work. You may think to yourself many times over, 'Why am I doing this? – I must be mad.' You may long for the familiarity of the weekly or monthly pay cheque; even for your old colleagues you were so relieved to say goodbye to, if you have already left. Keep your focus, concentrate on your long-term goals.

Summary

1. A focused, patient but thorough approach will help you land the job you want.
2. Be prepared for this to take time – use the time while you are waiting to strengthen your skills and knowledge base and to keep in touch with contacts, and, if you are going to a job that will command a lower salary, to boost your savings.

Summary exercises

1. Review your efforts to find work every week, set yourself goals for the following week.
2. Track those companies you have written to and not heard from.
3. Raise your profile at local events.

10 Starting and settling down

Settling down

Many people feel strange when they start a new career or even a new job. They yearn for what they are used to – the culture, the physical aspects of getting to work and knowing one's way round, how their colleagues work and socialize, familiar forms of behaviour and dress. In particular, you may miss certain clients coming on the phone to talk to you – you have to start at the beginning with new customers and form new relationships. You will not know who you can bounce ideas off and discuss issues, as your new colleagues size you up, perhaps wondering what changes you may implement. Plus, in your case, you are starting a new career. You have got extra things to get used to: a new culture, a different working environment and way of doing things. And you will almost certainly be landing in the middle of an organization that itself is undergoing changes. Embrace change.

There may be other things you have to get used to, such as:

- not rushing for the train in the morning;
- the buzz of a huge organization;
- the lack of bureaucracy;
- working under pressure – or not;
- lack of teamwork;
- not being a specialist.

Reconciling doubt

'Have I done the right thing?' is a natural question to ask yourself, especially in the first few weeks while everything is new and you are settling down. Give yourself time to adjust and compare the difference between the last sector you worked in and this new one; your last job and your new one. When you see how much of a difference there is between the two, you can sit back and tell yourself that it is only natural to wonder if you have done the right thing. Remember that you researched your career change and evaluated the options thoroughly before deciding it was the right thing to do. Your new employer believed you were the right person for the job. Recruiting is not cheap – it costs money, time and energy. They must have thought they were on to a sure thing. Show them. It is natural to long for the familiar when you have changed career. Think of your switch as an adventure – for which you are paid.

NEXT STEP

Relax and congratulate yourself.

Enjoy your career change! You have done it, you ought to be proud of yourself! Although increasing numbers of people are changing career now, it is still not an easy thing to do and you should congratulate yourself on your achievement. Walk tall! You have done it!

Now is the time to give yourself plenty of treats and pampering, and to celebrate your new career. You do not have to spend lots of money on doing so. You have got a lot to adjust to – and to prove to your new employer – so relax, and catch up with things you have wanted to do for ages, but have not had the time for. Get to know your new colleagues. Join in social events, contribute to birthday presents, ask others for their advice.

Now is also a good time to thank your family and supporters and show them how much you appreciated their help and support throughout the whole process.

NEXT STEP
Stay up with developments and grasp opportunities.

You had to convince people that you were the right person for the job when you were changing career and now it is important to show them that you are serious about what you are doing. Devote time – probably your own – to tracking developments in your sector on the Internet and in the press, trade and professional journals. Use any opportunity you can to discuss developments or interesting items, perhaps about competitors, with colleagues. Mention to people at work you have seen their name mentioned in the press. Make people feel good. They love it – view it as networking and furthering your working relationship with people.

You may decide to study for further qualifications – indeed, some employers may expect you to do so, and may help you train by:

- paying course fees and examination costs;
- giving you time off for study;
- paying the material costs such as books, videos, Internet access;
- providing live case studies for practical assignments and those that are relevant to the workplace.

NEXT STEP
Boost your employability and chances of remaining employed.

Invest in your survival skills. Work on your personal effectiveness. When you change career, your employer may provide continued training and help you develop in company time, but expect to develop your skills in your own time, and at your own expense. It is your future, so invest in it. Keep an eye out for courses on the Internet, at the local college, events your company or local professional body run, and ask to do them. Keep learning as much as you can in the practical, hands-on, on-the-job sense as well as the theory, and watching what competitors and product makers are doing.

If you belong to a professional body, join any special interest groups or focus groups in your area which provide forums for discussion. This could provide an opportunity for you to get involved in initiatives and make yourself known locally.

Constantly go the extra mile for people so that they always get more than they expect. If you give them a deadline, make sure it is one you can easily make so that your work is ready for them before they expect it.

ASK YOURSELF

What do I want to achieve next?

Now that you are actually doing the job, and getting a feel for it, consider whether there is scope to become an expert in your newly chosen field. Can you develop any particular expertise:

- Do you want to become the person who is interviewed by the local press when they are researching an article?
- Do you want to write books and articles about it?
- Do you want to be invited to give talks about it?
- Do you want to be the person people naturally think of when they need to know something?
- Do you want people to come from far and wide to ask for your help?
- How much of a geographic spread do you want this to cover?

This will raise your profile within your company and outside it; if you are running your own business, it can only help your prospects and reputation.

If you can impress customers and colleagues, you are more likely to find opportunities come your way. This is especially so if you get involved in local organizations and start taking on responsibilities that make a difference to those working in the sector. People will talk about you as a knowledgeable person who commands respect for what you do. Or do you just want to go in, do the job, and come away again? Get yourself known across the company and sector. Excel at what you do. Offer to help people and get involved and you will soon develop a strong network of contacts.

You will also need to think about your work–life balance, now that you are in the job and have an idea of what energy the working day takes and how involved you want to get beyond the immediate remit of the job. Be prepared too, once you have settled in, to take on responsibilities over and above any job description. Use any chance you have to raise your profile, both in the company and locally, but not at the expense of others. When invited to join groups, be friendly, listen rather than speak your mind bluntly, help out where you can and always deliver what you promise. Give people time to accept you. You are the newcomer; respect the experienced, and life will be easier and your new colleagues more welcoming. Show an interest, ask questions, get advice – and always thank people. You will advance much further.

If you can develop a niche, an area of expertise, where people seek your views, your future employment opportunities will be greatly enhanced. You may discover your niche once you have experience behind you and have had a chance to try out different areas.

ASK YOURSELF

How successful was my career change?

Rate your job satisfaction against your last job. Now that you are in your new career:

Are you MORE or LESS:

- Energetic?   More/Less
- Stressed about work in a positive way?   More/Less

- Enthusiastic about going to work? — More/Less
- Interested in what you are doing? — More/Less
- Inclined to read about your job after work? — More/Less
- Inclined to think positively about your job outside of working hours? — More/Less
- Happy with your lot? — More/Less
- Relaxed? — More/Less
- Better tempered? — More/Less
- Irritable? — More/Less
- In control of your life? — More/Less
- In tune with the people you work with because their values are similar to yours? — More/Less
- Have more time for interests outside of work? — More/Less
- Have less need for comfort things such as alcohol, chocolate, luxurious holidays, which made life more bearable before? — More/Less
- Confident in yourself? — More/Less
- Confident in your abilities to cope with change? — More/Less
- Keen to set another goal/more goals? — More/Less
- Finding you want to do more in the day? — More/Less

Talk to friends and family and ask them the same questions. Do they notice a change in you since you changed career?

ASK YOURSELF
What have I learnt about myself?

What have you learnt about yourself during this change? What particular qualities have you had to use? People who achieve goals need to be motivated, focused, determined and resourceful. Can you pick out the times when you were, and those periods when it all seemed to be a long way off? How did you cope with those? And what has that taught you about yourself? Can you relate that information to other examples of coping in your life? Are you inspired to instigate any other changes in your life? And could you use those qualities to help you achieve any other goals you want to meet, whether they be to lose weight, pay off that credit card, have a year out to go travelling in five year's time or set up your own business?

ASK YOURSELF
What have I learnt about the whole process of changing career?

Try to sit and think what you have learnt about the world of work in all this, and the business community, team working, the market, and what customers want. Try to think through the eyes of a business. Consider where you are headed and how you can make sure you achieve any further career goals you may have set yourself. Plot your skills development, so that you take the right paths to ensure you are always employed, by doing the correct courses and building on your own particular areas for development. Watch what is happening around you and consider how your role or business will be affected.

> **NEXT STEP**
>
> **Think ahead.**
> **Plan ahead.**

Some people do not like to plan ahead. They simply like to take life as it comes. That is fine, but the more alert you are, and the more control you have over your life, the more driven, motivated and happier you will be because you are living your life the way you want. Once you have settled into your new job and have had a chance to relax a bit – for example, six to nine months down the line:

1. Perform a complete financial and health 'MOT'.
2. Develop a five-year target of where you want to be and what you want to achieve.
3. See how far your network has expanded since you started your new career.
4. Review your strategy for how you would cope if you were suddenly made redundant. What would you do? How would you cope?
5. Watch the way you are spending your time. Are you spending the right amount of time on the things that matter to you?

Control the way you spend your time, and you are more likely to steer your efforts to things you want to do and be involved in – and make time for them. It will be easier to cut out the trivia.

Looking forward to the next change and enjoying life

Change has been going on for thousands of years in every aspect of life. Who would have thought 10 years ago that school girls under 16 would be able to get the morning-after pill in some schools in the UK? Or 100 years ago that we would be capable of building aircraft able to fly to Australia without stopping? List all the changes that have happened during the last century. Now think about what might come around in the next 10 years.

We are unable to predict change, which makes the whole thing all the more unsettling, threatening and unpredictable. Yet once you get into the way of thinking, self-reliance, self-worth and thinking and planning ahead, your belief in your ability to cope with change will rocket. There are far more opportunities around. Yes, the workplace is more risky ('Will I have a job next week?') but it is also a lot more fun and exciting with plenty of opportunities for those who want to get out there and take advantage of them.

Keep your career and life moving in a direction you want, and it will be much easier to embrace change and live life to the full.

Summary exercises

1. How would you like to see your job changing in the next year?
2. If you were to be made redundant tomorrow morning, what would your strategy be to get work?

Useful addresses and further information

Organizations that can help

Department for Education and Skills
www.dfes.gov.uk

IAG
www.myiag.org
This site will enable you to find an Information, Advice and Guidance Partnership in your area, which will be able to help you.

Qualifications and Curriculum Authority (QCA)
83 Piccadilly
London W1J 8QA
Tel: (020) 7509 5555
www.qca.org.uk

Scottish Qualifications Authority (SQA)
Hanover House
24 Douglas Street
Glasgow G2 7NQ
Help desk: (0141) 242 2214
www.sqa.org.uk

Equal opportunities

The Commission for Racial Equality
St. Dunstan's House
201–211 Borough High Street
London SE1 1GZ
Tel: (020) 7939 0000
www.cre.gov.uk

Equal Opportunities Commission
Arndale House
Arndale Centre
Manchester M4 3EQ
Tel: 0845 601 5901 for all general enquiries
www.eoc.org.uk

Returning to education, full- or part-time

BBC Learning Zone
www.bbc.co.uk/education

CACHE
Tel: (01727) 847636
www.cache.org.uk

City and Guilds & Affinity
1 Giltspur Street
London EC1A 9DD
Tel: (020) 7294 2800
www.city-and-guilds.co.uk

Edexcel
Customer Enquiries Unit
Stewart House
32 Russell Square
London WC1B 5DN
Tel: (0870) 240 9800
www.edexcel.org.uk

Floodlight
www.floodlight.co.uk
For courses in the London area.

Learn Direct, free information and advice on learning opportunities
and careers. Helpline number: (0800) 101 901
Visit their Web site at www.learndirect.co.uk

London Chamber of Commerce and Industry Examinations Board
Athena House
112 Station Road
Sidcup
Kent DA15 7BJ
Tel: (020) 8302 0261

National Extension College
The Michael Young Centre
Purbeck Road
Cambridge CB2 2HN
Tel: (01223) 400 200
www.nec.ac.uk
Provides a range of correspondence courses including GCSEs, A
levels, degrees and higher education, career and business skills,
counselling and guidance, leisure and interest and skills devel-
opment. Study in the comfort of your own home!

National Institute of Adult Continuing Education
20 Princess Road West
Leicester LE1 6TP
Tel: (0116) 204 4200/4201
www.niace.org.uk

Open College of the Arts
Unit 1B, Redbrook Business Park
Wilthorpe Road
Barnsley
South Yorkshire S75 1JN
Tel: (0800) 731 2116
www.oca-uk.com
They have a credit transfer arrangement with the Open University.
They offer courses in photography, creative writing, painting, drawing,
interior and garden design, music, singing, dance, sculpture, art history
and textiles.

Open University General Enquiries
PO Box 724
Milton Keynes
MK7 6ZS
Tel: (01908) 653231
www.open.ac.uk
It offers courses in arts and humanities, computing, English law, mathematics, environment, science, technology, business and management, education, health and social welfare, modern languages, psychology and social sciences.

Oxford, Cambridge and Royal Society for Arts (OCR)
Head Office
1 Regent Street
Cambridge CB2 1GG
Tel: (01223) 552552
www.ocr.org.uk

Pitman Qualifications
1 Giltspur Street
London EC1A 9DD
Tel: (020) 7294 3500

UCAS
Rosehill
New Barn Lane
Cheltenham
Gloucester GL52 3LZ
Tel: (01242) 222444 (general enquiries)
The Universities and Colleges Admissions Service. For details on university courses, visit their Web site: http://www.ucas.ac.uk

www.hotcourses.com
Has lots of information about courses, not just at undergraduate and postgraduate level, but also more generally throughout the country. If you are looking to acquire skills-based learning, this site is well worth a visit. It gives institutions, contact details and whether the courses are part-time, evening or day, or full-time, or distance learning.

I need help with...

The Basic Skills Agency
Commonwealth House
1–19 New Oxford Street
London WC1A 1NU
Tel: (020) 7405 4017
www.basic-skills.co.uk

Money

Career Development Loans
Tel: (0800) 585 505
(8.00 am to 10.00 pm, seven days a week)
www.lifelonglearning.co.uk

Department of Education, Student Support Branch
Rathgael House
43 Balloo Road
Bangor
County Down BT19 7PR
Tel: (0289) 127 9279
www.deni.gov.uk

Student Awards Agency for Scotland
Gyleview House
3 Redheughs Rigg
Edinburgh EH12 9HH
Tel:(0131) 476 8212
www.student-support-saas.gov.uk

Student Loans Company Ltd
100 Bothwell Street
Glasgow G2 7JD
Tel: (0800) 405010

Age issues

Employers Forum on Age
2nd Floor
The Tower Building
11 York Road
London SE1 7NX
Tel: (020) 7981 0341
www.efa.org.uk

The Pre-Retirement Association of Great Britain and Northern
Ireland
9 Chesham Road
Guildford
Surrey GU1 3LS
Tel: (01483) 301170
www.pra.uk.com
Runs courses in mid-life planning, helps people take stock and
make changes.

Being a recent graduate

C2: The Graduate Careers Shop
49 Gordon Square
London WC1H 0PN
Tel: (020) 7554 4555
www.careershop.co.uk

Childcare

Daycare Trust
21 St George's Road
London SE1 6ES
Tel: (020) 7840 3350
www.daycaretrust.org.uk
For help finding and choosing good-quality childcare.

Kids' Clubs Network
Tel: (020) 7512 2100
www.kidsclubs.com
For out of school clubs.

Parents at Work
1–3 Berry Street
London EC1V 0AA
Tel: (020) 7253 7243
Fax (020) 7253 6253
www.parentsatwork.org.uk

Dyslexia

British Dyslexia Association
98 London Road
Reading RG1 5AU
Tel: (0118) 966 8271
www.bda-dyslexia.org.uk

Lone parents

Child Support Agency national enquiry line
Tel: (08457) 133 133
www.dss.gov.uk/csa

Gingerbread
Tel: 0800 018 4318
www. gingerbread.org.uk

One Parent Families
Tel: (0800) 0185 026
www.oneparentfamilies.org.uk

Special needs

SKILL
Chapter House
18–20 Crucifix Lane
London SW1 3JW
Tel: (020) 7450 0620; information service: (0800) 328 5050;
minicom: (0800) 068 2422
www.skill.org.uk
Helps those with learning difficulties or disabilities.

Royal Association for Disability and Rehabilitation
12 City Forum
250 City Road
London EC1V 8AF
Tel: (020) 7250 3222
www.radar.org.uk

Royal National Institute for the Blind
RNIB Education and Employment Divisions
224 Great Portland Street
London W1N 2A
Helpline: (08457) 66 99 99
www.rnib.org.uk

Royal National Institute for the Deaf
19–23 Featherstone Street
London EC1Y 8SL
Tel: (0808) 808 0123 or (textphone only) (0808) 808 9000
www.rnid.org.uk
This organization can also give you details on British Sign Language
courses.

Running your own business

British Franchise Association
Thames View
Newtown Road
Henley-on-Thames

Oxon RG9 1HG
Tel: (01491) 578050
www.british-franchise.org
Offers help and advice in evaluating franchise offers, information guide and franchise manual for a fee.

Business Link (England)
  Tel: (0845) 600 9006;
Business Connect (Wales)
  Tel: (0845) 796 9798;
Business Shop (Scotland)
  Tel: (0845) 607 8787 from within Scotland or (0141) 228 2000 from anywhere within the UK
For an overview of the services offered:
www.businessadviceonline.org.uk

Direct Selling Association
29 Floral Street
Covent Garden
London WC2E 9DP
Tel: (020) 7497 1234
www.dsa.org.uk

Employer's Helpline
Tel: (0345) 143 143
Can help with basic tax matters or national insurance enquiries. Also provides basic information on registering for VAT, statutory sick pay and maternity benefit.

Federation of Small Businesses
Sir Frank Whittle Way
Blackpool Business Park
Blackpool
Lancs FY4 2FE
Tel: (01253) 336000
www.fsb.org.uk

Health and Safety Executive Information Line
HSE Infoline
Caerphilly Business Park
Caerphilly CF83 3GG
Tel: (08701) 545500
www.hse.gov.uk
Gives information and provides publications on a wide range of
business, health and safety issues.

Inland Revenue – general enquiries regarding tax matters PAYE,
expenses and benefits: call your local tax office for information.
Check your local phone book under 'Inland Revenue'.

Telework Association
WREN Telecottage
Stoneleigh Park
Warwickshire CV8 2RR
Tel: (02476) 696986
Helpline: (0800) 616008
www.tca.org.uk

www.namedroppers.com
Helpful if you want to check if the name of a company is still
available. You can also pick a name available connected with your
particular business.

Job hunting

If you want to check out jobs advertised on the Internet, try these
Web sites:

www.fish4.co.uk
www.getcareeralternatives.com
www.indepedent.co.uk
www.jobs4publicsector.com
www.jobsite.co.uk
www.charityconnections.co.uk
www.jobsunlimited.co.uk
www.manpower.co.uk

www.reed.co.uk
www.stepstone.co.uk
www.timesonline.co.uk
www.totaljobs.com
www.workthing.com

Getting information on specific careers

Accountancy

Association of Accounting Technicians
154 Clerkenwell Road
London EC1R 5AD
Tel: (020) 7837 8600
www.aat.co.uk

Association of Chartered Certified Accountants, Student
Recruitment and Training
64 Finnieston Square
Glasgow G3 8DT
Tel: (0141) 582 2000
www.accaglobal.com

Chartered Institute of Management Accountants
26 Chapter Street
London SW1P 4NP
Tel: (020) 7663 5441
www.cimaglobal.com

Chartered Institute of Public Finance and Accountancy
3 Robert Street
London WC2N 6RL
Tel: (020) 7543 5600
www.cipfa.org.uk

Institute of Chartered Accountants in England and Wales
Chartered Accountants' Hall
PO Box 433
London EC2P 2BJ
Tel: (020) 7920 8100
www.icaew.co.uk

Institute of Chartered Accountants of Scotland
21 Haymarkets Yard
Edinburgh EH12 5WS
Tel: (0131) 347 0100

Actuaries

Institute of Actuaries
Napier House
4 Worcester Street
Oxford OX1 2AW
Tel: (01865) 268200
www.actuaries.org.uk

Advertising

Advertising Association
Abford House
15 Wilton Road
London SW1V 1NJ
Tel: (020) 7828 2771
www.adassoc.org.uk

Chartered Institute of Marketing
Moor Hall
Cookham, Maidenhead
Berkshire SL6 9QH
Tel: (01628) 427500
www.cim.co.uk

Institute of Public Relations
The Old Trading House
15 Northburgh Street
London EC1V 0PR
Tel: (020) 7253 5151
www.ipr.org.uk

Institute of Sales and Marketing Management
Romeland House
Romeland Hill
St Albans
AL3 4ET
Tel: (01727) 812500
www.ismm.co.uk

Animals

The British Veterinary Association
7 Mansfield Street
London W1G 9NQ
Tel: (020) 7636 6541
www.bva.co.uk

British Veterinary Nursing Association
Suite 11
Shenval House
South Road
Harlow
Essex CM20 2BD
Tel: (01279) 450567
www.bvna.org.uk

Pet Care Trust
Bedford Business Centre
170 Mile Road
Bedford MK42 9TW
Tel: (01234) 273933
Provides leaflets on working in a pet shop and on dog grooming.
www.petcare.org.uk

RSPCA
Wilberforce Way
Southwater
Horsham RH13 9RS
Tel: (0870) 3335 999
www.rspca.org.uk

Banking

The Building Societies Association
3 Savile Row
London W1S 3PB
Tel: (020) 7437 0655
www.bsa.org.uk

The Chartered Institute of Bankers in Scotland
Drumsheugh House
38b Drumsheugh Gardens
Edinburgh EH3 7SW
Tel: (0131) 473 7777
www.ciobs.org.uk

The Chartered Insurance Institute
20 Aldermanbury
London EC2V 7HY
Tel: (020) 7417 4415/4416
www.cii.co.uk

The Institute of Financial Services
90 Bishopsgate
Tel: (01227) 762 600 (Administrative Centre)
Tel: (020) 7444 7111 (Registered Office)
www.ifslearning.co.uk

Association for Investment Management and Research
29th floor
One Canada Square
Canary Wharf
London E14 5DY
Tel: (020) 7712 1719
www.aimr.com

London Investment Banking Association
6 Frederick's Place
London EC2R 8BT
Tel: (020) 7796 3606
www.liba.org.uk

Building

Construction Industry Training Board
Bircham Newton
Kings Lynn
Norfolk PE31 6RH
Tel: (01485) 577577
www.citb.org.uk
For information on carpentry, joinery, builders.

Royal Institute of British Architects
Public Information Line
Tel: (0906) 302 0400
www.architecture.com

The Royal Institution of Chartered Surveyors
12 Great George Street
Parliament Square
London SW1P 3AD
Tel: (020) 7222 7000
www.rics.org.uk

Buyer/retail

The Chartered Institute of Purchasing and Supply
Easton House
Easton on the Hill
Stamford
Lincolnshire PE9 3NZ
Tel: (01780) 756777
www.cips.org

Careers guidance

Institute of Careers Guidance
Third Floor, Copthall House
1 New Road
Stourbridge
West Midlands DY8 1PH
Tel: (01384) 376464
www.icg-uk.org

Charity

Working for a Charity
The Peel Centre
Percy Circus
London WC1X 9EY
Tel: (020) 7833 8220
www.wfac.org.uk
Send an A4 SAE for information.

Children, working with

The National Youth Agency
17–23 Albion Street
Leicester LE1 6GD
Tel: (0116) 285 3700
www.nya.org.uk

Pre-School Learning Alliance
69 Kings Cross Road
London WC1X 9LL
Tel: (020) 7833 0991
www.pre-school.org.uk

The Church

Consult your own minister first.

Civil Service

www.cabinet-office.gov.uk
For information on England.

www.faststream.gov.uk
For the Fast Track Development Programme.

www.scotland.gov.uk
For the Scottish Executive.

www.wales.gov.uk
For the National Assembly for Wales.

Dentistry

The British Dental Association
64 Wimpole Street
London W1G 8YS
Tel: (020) 7935 0875
www.bda-dentistry.org.uk

Design

The Association of Photographers
81 Leonard Street
London EC2A 4QS
Tel: (020) 7739 6669
www.the-aop.org

The British Hat Guild
Unit E
Prince of Wales Business Park
Vulcan Street
Oldham
Lancs OL1 4ER
Tel: (0161) 627 4455
www.britishhatguild.co.uk

The Chartered Society of Designers
5 Bermondsey Exchange
179–181 Bermondsey Street
London SE1 3UW
Tel: (020) 7357 8088
www.csd.org.uk

The Crafts Council
44a Pentonville Road
Islington
London N1 9BY
Tel: (020) 7278 7700
www.craftscouncil.org.uk

The Design Council
34 Bow Street
London WC2E 7DL
Tel: (020) 7420 5200
www.design-council.org.uk

Institute of Engineering Designers
Courtleigh
Westbury Leigh, Westbury
Wiltshire BA13 3TA
Tel: (01373) 822801
www.ied.org.uk

Driving

Driving Instructors Association
Safety House
Beddington Farm Road
Croydon
Surrey CR0 4XZ
Tel: (020) 8665 5151 or 0845 345 5151
www.driving.org

Event planning

Association for Conferences and Events
ACE International
Riverside House
High Street
Huntingdon
Cambridgeshire PE18 6SG
Tel: (01480) 457595
www.martex.co.uk/ace

Funeral director

National Association of Funeral Directors
618 Warwick Road
Solihull
West Midlands B91 1AA
Tel: (0121) 711 1343
www.nafd.org.uk

Government

Convention of Scottish Local Authorities
Rosebery House
9 Haymarket Terrace
Edinburgh EH12 5XZ
Tel: (0131) 474 9200
www.cosla.gov.uk

Institute of Health Record Information and Management
www.ihrim.co.uk

The Trading Standards Institute
4–5 Hadleigh Business Centre
351 London Road
Hadleigh
Essex SS7 2BT
Tel: (0870) 872 9000
www.tradingstandards.gov.uk

Local government opportunities

Employers' Organisation for local government
Layden House
76–86 Turnmill Street
London EC1M 5LG
Tel: (020) 7296 6781
www.lg-employers.gov.uk

Health

Alternative Therapies
16 Duke's Wood Drive
Gerrards Cross
Bucks SL9 7LR
Tel: (01753) 890202

British Acupuncture Council
63 Jeddo Road
London W12 9HQ
Tel: (020) 8735 0400
www.acupuncture.org.uk

British Chiropractic Association
Blagrave House
17 Blagrave Street
Reading
Berkshire RG1 1QB
Tel: (0118) 950 5950
www.chiropractic-uk.co.uk

British College of Osteopathic Medicine
Lief House
120–122 Finchley Road
London NW3 5HR
Tel: (020) 7435 6464
www.bcno.ac.uk

British Dietetic Association
5th Floor
Charles House
148–9 Great Charles Streeet
Queensway
Birmingham B3 3HT
Tel: (0121) 200 8080
www.bda.uk.com

British Medical Association
BMA House
Tavistock Square
London WC1H 9JP
Tel: (020) 7387 4499
www.bma.org.uk

British Society of Audiology
80 Brighton Road
Reading
Berkshire RG6 1PS
Tel: (0118) 966 0622
www.b-s-a.demon.co.uk

British School of Osteopathy
275 Borough High Street
London SE1 1JE
Tel: (020) 7407 0222
www.bso.ac.uk

Chartered Institute of Environmental Health
Chadwick Court
15 Hatfields
London SE1 8DJ
Tel: (020) 7928 6006
www.cieh.org

Chartered Society of Physiotherapy
14 Bedford Row
London WC1R 4ED
Tel: (020) 7306 6666
www.csp.org.uk

College of Occupational Therapists
106–114 Borough High Street
Southwark
London SE1 1LB
Tel: (020) 7357 6480
www.cot.co.uk

The Society and College of Radiographers
207 Providence Square
Mill Street
London SE1 2EW
Tel: (020) 7740 7200
www.sor.org

Educational Kinesiology Foundation
16 Iris Road
West Ewell, Epsom
Surrey KT19 9NH
Tel: (020) 8391 5988
www.kinesiology.co.uk

The General Optical Council
41 Harley Street
London WIG 8DJ
Tel: (020) 7580 3898
www.optical.org

Institution of Occupational Health and Safety
The Grange
Highfield Drive
Wigston
Leicestershire LE18 1NN
Tel: (0116) 257 3100
www.iosh.co.uk

NHS Careers
Tel: (0845) 60 60 655
www.nhscareers.nhs.uk

Royal College of Speech and Language Therapists
2 White Hart Yard
London SE1 1NX
Tel: (020) 7378 1200
www.rcslt.org

The Royal Environmental Health Institute of Scotland
3 Manor Place
Edinburgh EH3 7DH
Tel: (0131) 225 6999
www.rehis.org

The Society of Homeopaths
4a Artizan Road
Northampton NN1 4HU
Tel: (01604) 621400
www.homeopathy-soh.org
www.naturopathy-uk.com
There are colleges of naturopathetic and complementary medicine
in London, Manchester, Dublin and Belfast, plus new ones to open
in 2001 in Edinburgh, Cork, Exeter and Galway.

Home economics

Institute of Consumer Sciences Incorporating Home Economics
Lonsdale House, 52 Blucher Street
Birmingham B1 1QU
Tel: (0121) 616 5188
ww.institute-consumer-sciences.co.uk

Horticulture

Institute of Groundsmanship
19–23 Church Street
The Agora
Wolverton
Milton Keynes MK12 5LG
Tel: (01908) 312511
www.iog.org.uk

Institute of Horticulture
14–15 Belgrave Square
London SW1X 8PS
Tel: (020) 7245 6943
www.horticulture.org.uk

The Landscape Institute
6–8 Barnard Mews
London SW11 1QU
Tel: (020) 7350 5200
www.l-i.org.uk

Royal Horticultural Society
80 Vincent Square
London SW1P 2PE
Tel: (020) 7834 4333
www.rhs.org.uk

Hospitality

Hospitality Training Foundation
International House
High Street
London W5 5DB
Tel: (020) 8579 2400
www.htf.org.uk

Hotel and Catering International Management Association
Trinity Court
34 West Street
Sutton
Surrey SM1 1SH
Tel: (020) 8661 4900
www.hcima.org.uk

The Institute of Brewing
33 Clarges Street
London W1J 7EE
Tel: (020) 7499 8144

National Association of Master Bakers
21 Baldock Street
Ware
Hertfordshire SG12 9DH
Tel: (01920) 468061
www.masterbakers.co.uk

Housing

British Association of Removers
3 Churchill Court
58 Station Road
North Harrow
Middlesex HA2 7SA
Tel: (020) 8861 3331
www.removers.org.uk

Institute of Logistics and Transport
11–12 Buckingham Gate
London SW1E 6LB
Tel: (01536) 740 100
www.iolt.org.uk

National Association of Estate Agents
Arbon House
21 Jury Street
Warwick CV34 4EH
Tel: (01926) 496800
www.naea.co.uk

IT

The British Computer Society
1 Sanford Street
Swindon
Wiltshire SN1 1HJ
Tel: (01793) 417417
www.bcs.org.uk

British Interactive Media Association (BIMA)
Briarlea House
Southend Road
South Green
Billericay CM11 2PR
Tel: (01277) 658107
www.bima.co.uk

Information Technology National Training Organization
1 Castle Lane
London SW1 6DR
Tel: (020) 7580 6677

Institute of Management Services
Stowe House, Netherstowe
Lichfield
Staffordshire, WS13 6TJ
Tel: (01543) 251346
www.ims-productivity.com

The National Computing Centre Limited
Oxford House
Oxford Road
Manchester M1 7ED
Tel: (0161) 242 2121
www.ncc.co.uk

Skillset – the National Training Organization for Broadcast, Film,
Video and Interactive Media
Prospect House
80–110 New Oxford Street
London WC1A 1HB
Tel: (020) 7520 5757
www.skillset.org

Journalism

College of Technical Authorship
PO Box 7
Cheadle
Cheshire SK8 3BY
Tel: (0161) 437 4235
www.coltecha.com

National Council for the Training of Journalists
Latton Bush Centre
Southern Way
Harlow
Essex CM18 7BL
Tel: (01279) 430009
www.nctj.com

Society for Editors and Proofreaders
Putney Bridge Approach, Fulham
London SW8 3JD
Tel: (020) 7736 3278
www.sfep.org.uk

Languages

Institute of Translation and Interpreting
Fortuna House
South Fifth Street
Milton Keynes
Tel: (01908) 325250
www.iti.org.uk

Legal

General Council of the Bar
2–3 Cursitor Street
London EC4A 1NE
Tel: (020) 7440 4000
www.barcouncil.org.uk

Institute of Barristers' Clerks
2–3 Cursitor Street
London EC4A 1NE
Tel: (020) 7831 7144
www.barristersclerks.com

Institute of Paralegal Training
The Mill
Clymping Street
Clymping
Littlehampton
West Sussex BN17 5RN
Tel: (01903) 714276

The Law Society
Tel: (0870) 606 2555
www.lawsociety.org.uk

Leisure

Booksellers Association of Great Britain and Ireland
Minster House
272–274 Vauxhall Bridge Road
London SW1V 1BA
Tel: (020) 7802 0802
www.booksellers.org.uk

British Casino Association
38 Grosvenor Gardens
London SW1W 0EB
Tel: (020) 7730 1055
www.britishcasinoassociation.org.uk

British Institute of Innkeeping
Wessex House
80 Park Street
Camberley
Surrey GU15 3PT
Tel: (01276) 684449
wwwbii.org.uk

Institute of Leisure and Amenity Management
ILAM House
Lower Basildon
Reading
Berkshire RG8 9NE
Tel: (01491) 874800
www.ilam.co.uk

Institute of Sport and Recreation Management
Sir John Beckwith Centre for Sport
Loughborough University
Loughborough
Leicestershire LE11 3TU
Tel: (01509) 226474
www.isrm.co.uk

Institute of Travel and Tourism
Mill Studio
Crane Mead
Ware
Hertfordshire SG12 9PY
Tel: (0870) 770 7960
www.itt.co.uk

Pianoforte Tuners' Association
c/o 10 Reculver Road
Herne Bay
Kent CT6 6LD
Tel: (01227) 368808
www.pianotuner.org.uk

Retail Department
Brewers & Licensed Retailers Association
42 Portman Square
London W1H 0BB
Tel: (020) 7486 4831

The Travel and Tourism and Events Sector National Training
Organization
12–18 Claremont Road
West Byfleet
Surrey KT14 6DY
Tel: (01932) 345835

Wine and Spirit Education Trust
Five King's House
1 Queen Street Place
London EC4R 1QS
Tel: (020) 7236 3551
www.wset.co.uk

Library/Information Services

Chartered Institute of Library and Information Professionals (CILIP)
7 Ridgmount Street
London WC1E 7AE
Tel: (020) 7255 0500
www.cilip.org.uk

Management and administration

AMSPAR (Association of Medical Secretaries, Practice Managers
Administrators and Receptionists Ltd)
Tavistock House North
Tavistock Square
London WC1H 9LN
Tel: (020) 7387 6005
www.amspar.co.uk

Chartered Institute of Taxation
12 Upper Belgrave Street
London SW1X 8BB
Tel: (020) 7235 9381
www.tax.org.uk

Institute of Administrative Management
16 Park Crescent
London W1B 1BA
Tel: (020) 7612 7099
www.instam.org

Institute of Agricultural Secretaries and Administrators Ltd
National Agricultural Centre
Stoneleigh
Kenilworth
Warwickshire CV8 2LZ
Tel: (02476) 696592
www.iagsa.co.uk

Institute of Chartered Secretaries and Administrators (ICSA)
16 Park Crescent
London W1B 1AH
Tel: (020) 7580 4741
www.icsa.org.uk

Institute of Management
2 Savoy Court
The Strand
London WC2R OEZ
Tel: (020) 7497 0580
www.inst-mgt.org.uk

Institute of Management Consultancy
3rd Floor
17–18 Hayward's Place
London EC1R 0EQ
Tel: (020) 7566 5220
www.imc.co.uk

Chartered Institute of Personnel and Development
CIPD House
Camp Road
London SW19 4UX
Tel: (020) 8971 9000
www.cipd.co.uk

Recruitment and Employment Confederation
36–38 Mortimer Street
London W1W 7RG
Tel: (020) 7462 3260
www.rec.uk.com

Royal Statistical Society
12 Errol Street
London EC1Y 8LX
Tel: (020) 7638 8998
www.rss.org.uk

Museum/history

The British Association of Paintings Conservator-Restorers
PO Box 32
Hayling Island
PO11 9WE
Tel: (0239) 246 5115
www.abpr.co.uk

British Antique Dealers' Association
20 Rutland Gate
London SW7 1BD
Tel: (020) 7589 4128
www.bada.org

Council for British Archaelology
Bowes Morrell House
111 Walmgate
York YO1 9WA
Tel (01904) 671417
www.britarch.ac.uk

Cultural Heritage National Training Organisation
7 Burnett Street
Little Germany
Bradford BD1 5BJ
Tel: (01274) 391056
www.chnto.co.uk

Institute of Field Archaeologists
University of Reading
2 Earley Gate
PO Box 239
Reading
Berkshire RG6 6AU
Tel: (0118) 931 6446
www.archaeologists.net

The Museums Association
24 Calvin Street
London E1 6NW
Tel: (020) 7426 6970
www.museumsassociation.org

United Kingdom Institute for Conservation of Historic and Artistic
Works
109 The Chandlery
50 Westminster Bridge Road
London SE1 7QY
Tel: (020) 7721 8721
www.ukic.org.uk

Performing arts

Access to Music
18 York Road
Leicester LE1 5TS
Tel: (0800) 281 842
www.access-to-music.co.uk

British Actors Equity Association
Guild House
Upper St Martin's Lane
London WC2H 9EG
Tel: (020) 7379 6000
www.equity.org.uk

British Association for Drama Therapists
41 Broomhouse Lane
London SW6 3DP
Tel: (020) 7731 0160
www.badth.ision.co.uk

The British Association of Art Therapists
Southampton Place Business Centre
16–19 Southampton Place
London WC1A 2AJ
Tel: (020) 7745 7262
www.baat.org

BBC Recruitment Services
www.bbc.co.uk.jobs

British Society for Music Therapy
61 Church Hill Road, East Barnet
Hertfordshire EN4 8SY
Tel: (020) 8441 6226
www. bsmt.org

The Incorporated Society of Musicians
10 Stratford Place
London W1C 1AA
Tel: (020) 7629 4413
www.ism.org

National Council for Drama Training
1–7 Woburn Walk
London WC1H 0JJ
Tel: (020) 7387 3650
www.ncdt.co.uk

Royal Academy of Dramatic Art
62–64 Gower Street
London WC1E 6ED
Tel: (020) 7636 7076
www.rada.org

Skillset – the National Training Organization for Broadcast, Film, Video and Interactive Media. See page 213 for full details.
www.thestage.co.uk
Information and advice about the acting profession.

Printing

Institute of Printing
The Mews, Hill House
Clanricarde Road
Tunbridge Wells
Kent TN1 1NU
Tel: (01892) 538118
www.instituteofprinting.org

Psychology

Association of Educational Psychologists
26 The Avenue
Durham DH1 4ED
Tel: (0191) 384 9512
www.aep.org.uk

The British Psychological Society
St Andrews House
48 Princess Road East
Leicester LE1 7DR
Tel: (0116) 254 9568
www.bps.org.uk

Publishing

The Publishers Association
29B Montague Street
London WC1B 5BH
Tel: (020) 7691 9191
www.publishers.org.uk

Society of Authors
84 Drayton Gardens
London SW10 9SB
Tel: (020) 7373 6642
www.writers.org.uk/society

Society for Editors and Proofreaders
Putney Bridge Approach
Fulham
London SW8 3JD
Tel: (020) 7736 3278
www.sfep.org.uk

The Society of Indexers
Blades Enterprise Centre
John Street
Sheffield S2 4SU
Tel: (0114) 292 2350
www.socind.demon.co.uk

Science

The Association of Clinical Biochemists
130–132 Tooley Street
London SE1 2TU
Tel: (020) 7403 8001
www.acb.org.uk

The Institute of Biology
20 Queensberry Place
London SW7 2DZ
Tel: (020) 7581 8333
www.iob.org

Institute of Biomedical Science
12 Coldbath Square
London EC1R 5HL
Tel: (020) 7713 0214
www.ibms.org

The Royal Society of Chemistry
Burlington House
London W1J 0BA
Tel: (020) 7437 8656
www.rsc.org

Society

British Security Industry Association Limited
Security House
Barbourne Road
Worcester WR1 1RS
Tel: (01905) 21464
www.bsia.co.uk

Metropolitan Police Service
Recruitment and Selection Centre
New Scotland Yard
Victoria Street
London SW1
Tel: (0845) 727 2212
www.met.police.uk

Police Division
Scottish Office Home Department
Room E1–7
Saughton House
Broomhouse Drive
Edinburgh EH11 3XD

Police Recruiting Department
Tel: (0845) 608 3000
www.policecouldyou.co.uk

224

Prison Officers' Association
Tel: (020) 8803 0255
www.poauk.org.uk

Security Industry Training Organization
Security House
Barbourne Road
Worcester WR1 1RS
Tel: (01905) 20004
www.sito.co.uk

Teaching

Association of University Teachers
Egmont House
25–31 Tavistock Place
London WC1H 9UT
Tel: (020) 7670 9700
www.aut.org.uk

Graduate Teacher Training Registry
Rosehill
New Barn Lane
Cheltenham
Gloucestershire GL52 3LZ
Tel: (0870) 1122205
www.gttr.ac.uk

Independent Schools Council Information Service
Grosvenor Gardens House
35–37 Grosvenor Gardens
London SW1W 0BS
Tel: (020) 7798 1560
www.iscis.uk.net

The Teacher Training Agency: campaign to get high-quality
graduates into teaching
Tel: (0845) 600 0991
www.canteach.gov.uk

Transport

Civil Aviation Authority
CAA House
45–59 Kingsway
London WC2B 6TE
Tel: (020) 7379 7311
www.caa.co.uk

Licensed Taxi Drivers Association
Taxi House
Woodfield Road
London W9 2BA
Tel: (020) 7286 1046
www.itda.co.uk

Volunteering

Community Service Volunteers (CSV)
237 Pentonville Road
London N1 9NJ
Tel: (020) 7278 6601
www.csv.org.uk

TimeBank
The Mezzanine
Elizabeth House
39 York Road
London SE1 7NQ
Tel: (020) 7401 5420
www.timebank.org.uk

Voluntary Service Overseas
www.vso.org.uk
VSO, a charity established in 1948 to enable Britons to employ their
skills in poorer nations.

Further reading

Courses

The University and College Entrance Guide: The Official Guide (annual) available from bookshops and careers libraries. Lists all the courses available and the sorts of qualifications you need to get in

Financial Support for Higher Education Students; produced by the
 Department for Employment and Skills

Hunting for that job

Greenwood, D (1999) *The Job Hunter's Handbook*, Kogan Page,
 London

Handy, C, Handy, E (1999) *The New Alchemists... How Visionary
 People Make Something out of Nothing*, Hutchinson, London

Krechowiecka, Irene (2000) *Net that Job*, Kogan Page, London

McGee, P (1999) *Writing a CV that Works*, How To Books Ltd,
 Oxford

Nickell, H (2002) *Surfing Your Career*, How To Books Ltd, Oxford

Vandevelde, H (1999) *Harnessing Technology for Career Success:
 from Online CV to Digital Interview*, Trotman and Company,
 Richmond

Yate, M-J (2001) *Great Answers to Tough Interview Questions*, Kogan Page, London

Specific jobs

Occupations, published annually by COIC and available in careers services and public libraries. A mine of information, with useful entry for late starters for each career, together with details of professional bodies to whom you can write for more information

Krechowiecka, I (2002) *The Times A–Z of Careers and Jobs*, 9th edn, Kogan Page, London

Working for yourself

Barrow, C, Golzen, G, and Kogan, H (2000) *The Daily Telegraph Guide to Taking up a Franchise*, Kogan Page, London

Golzen, G, and Kogan, H (2000) *The Daily Telegraph Guide to Working for Yourself*, Kogan Page, London

Other

Brown, S (2003) *Moving On Up*, Ebury Press, London

Index